T0319161

Chinese Publishing

As the birthplace of printing, China has some claim to being the homeland of publishing. China's ancient civilization has nurtured a distinctively Chinese publishing industry, and this industry has done much to spread Chinese ideas and culture around the world. Yang Hu and Xiao Yang provide a comprehensive introduction to the origins and development of printing and publication in China from ancient to modern times, complemented throughout with full color illustrations.

Introductions to Chinese Culture

The thirty volumes in the Introductions to Chinese Culture series provide accessible overviews of particular aspects of Chinese culture written by a noted expert in the field concerned. The topics covered range from architecture to archaeology, from mythology and music to martial arts. Each volume is lavishly illustrated in full color and will appeal to students requiring an introductory survey of the subject, as well as to more general readers.

Yang Hu
Xiao Yang

CHINESE
PUBLISHING

CAMBRIDGE
UNIVERSITY PRESS

CAMBRIDGE
UNIVERSITY PRESS

University Printing House, Cambridge CB2 8BS, United Kingdom

One Liberty Plaza, 20th Floor, New York, NY 10006, USA

477 Williamstown Road, Port Melbourne, VIC 3207, Australia

314-321, 3rd Floor, Plot 3, Splendor Forum, Jasola District Centre, New Delhi - 110025, India

79 Anson Road, #06-04/06, Singapore 079906

Cambridge University Press is part of the University of Cambridge.

It furthers the University's mission by disseminating knowledge in the pursuit of education, learning and research at the highest international levels of excellence.

www.cambridge.org
Information on this title: www.cambridge.org/9780521186759

Originally published by China Intercontinental Press as
Chinese Publishing (9787508513157) in 2010

© China Intercontinental Press 2010

This updated edition is published by Cambridge University Press
with the permission of China Intercontinental Press under
the China Book International programme 👁.

For more information on the China Book International programme, please visit
http://www.cbi.gov.cn/wisework/content/10005.html

Cambridge University Press retains copyright in its own contributions
to this updated edition

© Cambridge University Press 2012

First published 2012

A catalogue record for this publication is available from the British Library

ISBN 978-0-521-18675-9 Paperback

Contents

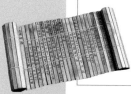

Preface: Three Thousand Years of Books in China

China's ancient civilization has nurtured a distinctive Chinese publishing industry, with both continuity and innovation. Publishing, a significant cultural activity, has contributed greatly to the spread of Chinese civilization. Moreover, as one of the first countries to develop an advanced publishing industry, ancient China played an important role in the global history of publishing. Over thousands of years, Chinese civilization has spread all over the world through books. The invention of papermaking and printing techniques in China and their spread have profoundly influenced the development of human society.

The written language is the prerequisite for a publishing industry. China has had many different nationalities and languages since ancient times. However, among all the written languages of the ancient civilizations, Chinese had a continuous, stable character outline. Because of the continuity of the Chinese written language, people today can understand different kinds of books written thousands years ago in China and fluently depict today's fast developing world.

After the appearance of written language as a carrier of knowledge, the problem for the development of the publishing industry was to find the appropriate material on which to record information. After trying bamboo, wood, bone, bronze, stone and silk, the Chinese people invented paper around the second century B.C.

In 105 A.D., the gradual spread of papermaking techniques, innovated by Cai Lun, promoted the development of publishing and society. Inspired by rubbing and sealing techniques, Chinese people invented printing techniques in the seventh century B.C. This led to progress in the quality and quantity of book publishing and brought human communication to a new stage. During 1041–1049 A.D., the civilian Bi Sheng invented typography, the printing-type which transferred from plaster to wood to metal such as copper or tin. In the eleventh century, registration printing came into being on the basis of engraving, which made printed matter more attractive and plentiful.

From the twenty-first century B.C. to the sixteenth century B.C., Chinese publishing was burgeoning and developing. Primary editions and classical collections appeared. It is conservatively estimated that the Chinese publishing industry has a history of over 3,000 years.

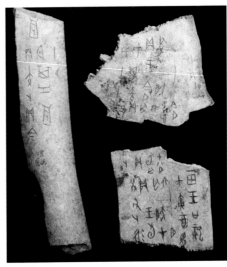

Oracle bone pieces with inscriptions

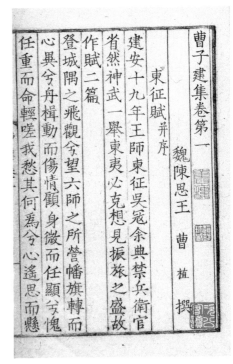

Bronze movable-type print from the Ming Dynasty (1368–1644)—*Cao Zijian's Collection*

   Early compilation activities followed, in which Chinese people accumulated rich compiling experience and developed their own compiling methods. The invention of papermaking, which later become a major category of Chinese handicraft, fundamentally changed the media of written language.

   Five major publishing systems were gradually established after the appearance of printing techniques: official publications from government publishing houses; bookshop publications from private publishing houses; personal publications; academic publications from academic publishing houses and temple and monastery publications. The boom of the publishing industry promoted book circulation and trade. In the second century B.C., *Shu Si* (书肆), early book marketplaces, came in to existence in

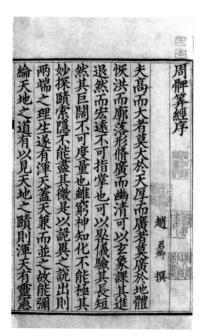

Jianyang copy of *Zhou Bi Suan Jing*, from the Song Dynasty (960–1279).

Brand mark of *The Kai Feng Story*, from the Song Dynasty

Chang'an and other economically and culturally developed cities. Book businesses gradually flourished during the Tang and Song dynasties (618–1279) and various business methods including advertising were used. During the Southern Song Dynasty (1127–1279), the idea and practice of copyright entered the Chinese book industry. The earliest copyright mark was in the brand mark of the book *The Kai Feng Story* 《东都事略》 (published in 1190–1194), on which fifteen characters were written, reading "first published by Cheng from Mt. MeiShan, registered already, no unauthorized copy is allowed."

China has a fine tradition of "valuing knowledge and honoring writing." Since ancient times, Chinese intellectuals have devoted themselves to writing to express faith and earn fame. Statistics show that there are some 2.3 million volumes of 180,000 different

An illustration from a secret copy of *Bei Xi Xiang* published in the thirteenth year of Emperor Chong Zhen in the Ming Dynasty (1639)

kinds surviving from the Western Han Dynasty to the Qing Dynasty (202 B.C.–1911 A.D.). Ancient Chinese books have various categories. Under Confucian classics, history, philosophy, literature,

Books with different layouts published by governmental organizations in the Qing Dynasty (1644–1911)

Buddhist and Taoist scriptures, there are diverse types of literature. Giant works with many volumes symbolize the grandeur of ancient Chinese literature and the prosperity of the publishing industry. Great works like the *Yongle Encyclopedia* of the Ming Dynasty (1368–1644, with 370 million words), *The Compendium of Works of Past and Present* of the Qing Dynasty (1644–1911), the *Imperial Collection of Four* (nearly one billion words) were the classics. Chinese books, particular about beauty in form, have bamboo and wooden slips, scroll and album book systems with various bookbinding forms consisting of folding, whirlwind binding, dragon-scale binding, butterfly-like binding, wrapped-ridge binding and traditional thread binding. In addition, Chinese books have elegant regard for paper and ink, style, and format.

Cherishing books and old scriptures is one of the fine traditions in Chinese culture. But owing to both human and natural factors, many ancient books have been lost, stirring even greater efforts in collecting and protecting books.

Book collections have a long history in China. Collecting systems evolved among feudal officials, private persons,

Buddhist and Taoist temples and academies of classical learning. In ancient China, there were millions of private libraries and bibliophiles contributed to book maintenance, repairing and protection. As a result, a distinct book-keeping culture has developed.

China, historically, has stressed communication with other countries. Publication exchanges are an important means of communication. "The Book Road" was built across Asia and Europe during long periods of cross-cultural communication. As a result, China has spread its advanced publishing technique together with its science and culture, and also learned from other countries and areas.

Although Chinese publishing led the world for a long time and exerted widespread influence, especially in the publishing industries of countries in the "Confucian Civilization circle,"

Library of Yue Lu Academy in Hunan Province: the Yu Shu Building

Book Disaster
This refers to man-made damage to officially collected books in ancient China. As early as the Sui Dynasty, Niu Hong had a view of "Five Disasters": the first was "Burning books" by Qin Shihuang in the Qin Dynasty; the second was the "Chimei" rebellion army entering the Central Plains at the end of West Han Dynasty; the third "Dongzhuo shifting capital" in the Three Kingdoms Period; the fourth Liu (Liu Yuan) and Shi(Shi Le)'s Rebellion in Northern and Southern Dynasties; the fifth "Burning books" in Jiangling by Emperor Yuan of Liang in the Sothern Dynasty. Later, in the Ming Dynasty, Hu Yinglin added another five: the sixth was "Burning books" in Jiangdu at the end of the Sui Dynasty; the seventh the "An Lushan Rebellion" in the Tang Dynasty; the eighth "Huangchao entering Chang'an" at the end of the Tang Dynasty; the ninth "the Humiliation of Jingkang" in North Song Dynasty; the tenth the destruction of the Song Dynasty by Mongolia. These ten are called the "Ten Disasters."

the influence of Chinese publishing has decreased in modern times.

From the nineteenth century onwards, with western learning spreading to the east, the Chinese publishing industry has drawn lessons from western-developed publishing.

Founded in 1897 and 1912 respectively, the Commercial Press and Zhonghua Book Company have become publishing companies keeping abreast of the times by actively improving technology and adopting market principles. In the first half of the twentieth century, the Chinese publishing industry was revolutionized and emerged into the world publishing industry with a brand-new outlook. From then on, Chinese publishing has entered into a splendid period of development. China has become a power in the global publishing industry.

First, the scale of the publishing industry is growing. In 1950, there were 211 publishing houses in China and 12,153 kinds of books with total printing runs of 275 million volumes per year. However, in 2007, there were 578 publishing houses and 248,283 kinds of books with the total annual print runs of 6.293 billion volumes.

According to predictions in *A Study on the System of Development Index of the Publishing Industry in a Well-off Society* by the China Institute of Publishing Science, the value of the Chinese publishing industry will reach RMB800 billion by 2020, accounting to 1.9–2.0% of GDP, printing 8.198 billion volumes per year.

Second, publishing technology is developing daily and digital publishing is booming. Combining computer technology with Chinese

An edition of *An Outline Treatise of Medical Herbs* (《本草纲目》), published in Japan at the turn of the seventeenth century.

character printing, the Chinese character laser photo-typesetting technique helps the Chinese printing industry step into the future. Meanwhile, featuring a single volume as the minimum print run and with the goal of meeting personalized requirements, printing on demand (POD) has become a new publication model. The development of digital technology is influencing the Chinese publishing industry profoundly. Today's Chinese publishing market mainly consists of paper, online and mobile phone publications.

Third, commercialization and the legal system in the publishing sector have advanced. The development of new technology and the globalization of the Chinese market are changing the development model of Chinese publishing. Due to the changes taking place, most publishing institutions are developing of modern company culture.

In the field of circulation, publishing channels such as non-state-operated bookshops, online bookshops and book clubs are rising. With constant improvements to the legal system affecting press and publications, a legal system framework centering on the Copyright Law has taken shape and the law enforcement

Hand flatbed press, used by Shanghai Newspaper Press (Shenbaoguan) in 1872.

system for judicial and administrative protection has been formulated.

Fourth, publishing is becoming increasingly international and the copyright trade is developing rapidly. After entering into the twenty-first century, China's publishing industry has made remarkable achievements in copyright business and co-publishing. It not only actively introduces excellent books from abroad, but also successfully releases many publications about ancient Chinese civilization and contemporary Chinese culture. In the past ten years, the structure of copyright business in China has improved every year. The ratio of input to output was close to 5:1 in 2007 comparing to the 15:1 ten years ago. Furthermore, Chinese publishers frequently attend international book fairs, including book fairs in Frankfurt, London and the US. The international impact of the yearly Beijing International Book Fair is greater each year. It is worth mentioning that the 2009 Frankfurt International Book Fair, hailed as the most significant in the world, has seen China emerge as the main exhibitor. With

"Zhonghua Women" founded by Zhonghua Book Company. In the beginning of the twentieth century, modern publishing in China presented an appearance of prosperity marked by the large scale publishing of magazines.

over 7,600 kinds of exhibits, there were numerous Chinese publishing houses at the fair including 272 from mainland China, 26 from Taiwan and 15 from Hong Kong. According to German official statistics, China is now the main exhibitor and has drawn 290,000 visitors. It has effectively accelerated the development of Chinese publishing.

Since the twentieth century, it is not only the publishing industry on the Chinese mainland that has expanded rapidly, but also the publishing industries in Taiwan, Hong Kong and Macao. Based on co-prosperity and development, the publishing industries in all these places create a pattern of "diversity in unity" of the Chinese-language publishing industry. With a driving development trend that matches China's ancient publishing industry, they occupy a fundamental position in today's global publishing industry.

The outstanding features of the Chinese publishing industry are rooted in characteristics of Chinese culture: "classics in the past, innovation in the present." Its main features can be illustrated as follows:

Some of the numerous visitors in the "Classic and Innovation" pavilions in the China Section of the Frankfurt International Book Fair 2009.

(1) Time-honored history. China, as one of the four ancient civilizations of the world, was one of the first countries to start publishing activities. Chinese publishing has been evolving over 3,000 years.

(2) Rich content. Long-standing publishing activities preserve precious historical cultural heritage for today's China and the world. The development and revolution of printing technology, and its transmission, consistency and extent, are worthy of note.

(3) Unity in diversity. "Diversity" means that the publishing industry has flourished across China; and "unity" indicates that the main content of various ethnic groups' publishing industries still show Chinese civilization including Confucianism, Buddhism and Taoism.

(4) Profound influence. China's publishing industry has not only influenced the formation and development of Chinese civilization, but also significantly contributes to the development of the publishing industry around the world. Its outstanding embodiments are the extensive prevalence of papermaking and printing technology as well as the formation of a civilization zone in East Asia.

(5) Constant innovation. Chinese publishing has continuously developed and innovated. Chinese publishing culture boasts entrepreneurship, illustrated by independent innovation (papermaking and printing technology) and the absorption and fusion of other cultures (the introduction of Buddhism, the acceptance of western culture into China).

This book depicts the development and overall features of Chinese publishing, running through a remarkable history of over 3,000 years.

A Long-Standing and Well-Established History

The Origin and Development of China's Ancient Publishing Industry

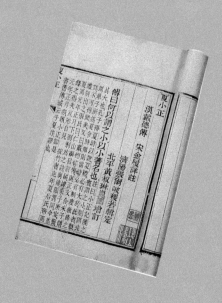

The Xia Dynasty, established in 2070 B.C., was the first dynasty in China and marked the beginning of a new era in Chinese civilization. There is evidence to show that Chinese writing had developed and was on its way to being systemized at this time. Chinese ancestors also developed a degree of aesthetic and cultural accomplishment. The appearance of primary writing tools and books paved the way for early publishing activities.

The Origin of Chinese Characters

The Chinese character is an important marker of humanity's shift from pre-literate to literate times. Written language is the basis of human civilization because it can be passed down through time and space. Chinese characters played a decisive role in the development of Chinese culture and the publishing industry.

The development of Chinese characters was a long process that can be divided into two periods before their final appearance. One is the time when the spoken language existed without a written language. The other is that of a written language without complete articles. On the basis of language and objectives, the real emergence of Chinese characters underwent three stages during which events were recorded by knotted cords, carvings and graphs.

Cangjie, a legendary figure in ancient China (2600 B.C.), claimed to be an official historian

Portrait of Cangjie.

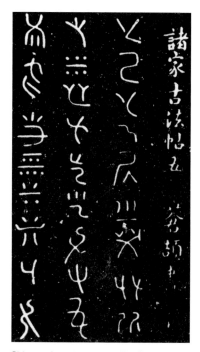

Chinese characters created by Cangjie according to legend.

of the Yellow Emperor and the inventor of the Chinese character. According to legend he had four eyes to observe all things on earth. Historical records show that Chinese characters had already been invented by Cangjie's time. By then, a certain number of characters were in use. Therefore, some scholars hold the view that Chinese characters had already been created but did not have any fixed style, and that Cangjie's contribution was to unify and standardize them.

Knotting cords to record events, carved inscriptions, graphs and graphic symbols were the four important steps that led to the invention of the written language, according to historical documents and archaeological finds. Among these, graphic symbols or pictographic writing were most influential. Pictographic writing appeared in the later period of primitive society, namely the high days of the New Stone Age. Pictographic features can be found in many ethnic minority languages in China. A typical one is the *Dongba Classics* of the Naxi people in Yunnan Province. Graphic symbols from the *Classics* were gradually developed into pictographic language.

Similar graphic symbols and writings are found among the Yangshao culture of 4000 B.C. and the Longshan Cultural Relics, which came later. Some eighteen graphic symbols were found

Dongba Classics.

on the potteries of Ling Yanghe and Dazhu villages in Shandong Province. Four of them are pictured here:

Graphic symbols carved on the pottery found in Dawenkou.

Many scholars consider these graphic symbols to be written language from the later period of the Dawenkou culture (about 2800–2500B.C.). Nevertheless, more and more archaeological discoveries suggest that the Longshan Culture existed 4,500 years ago. The period is also that of the Huangdi legend. It was around this time that Chinese characters essentially changed from rudimentary and began to take shape.

Archaeological finds show that writing tools existed before the invention of the written language. The Banpo pottery inscriptions have several designs similar to a human face, swimming fish and the ✳ pattern. They were drawn with writing brushes or other

Pottery inscription of the Xia dynasty found in Erlitou, Henan Province.

similar tools. The writings are clear and distinguishable. The pottery inscriptions found in Dawenkou, Shandong Province in 1959 include both carving and writing, which means that simple carving and writing tools were available at the time. The writing brush began to take on the features of the pen no later than during the Shang Dynasty.

With more expressive features, the carapace-bone-script emerged during the Shang Dynasty (1600–1046 B.C.) after a long period of evolution from the earliest characters. It is the earliest mature and systematic group of Chinese characters that

A writing brush unearthed in Wuwei, Gansu Province. The writing brush was a basic writing tool in ancient China. It is still used by many people today.

The evolution of Chinese characters.

can be seen today. After the oracle bone inscriptions, a variety of fonts, comprising bronze script, large seal script, small seal script, clerical script and regular script, appear throughout Chinese history. When it came to regular script, the grapheme - or smallest significant unit in a writing system - of Chinese characters, still in use today, was basically finalized.

Based on the premise of definite and clear meaning, the general evolution of Chinese characters has been from complexity to simplicity. As a result, the pictographic characters originally used have been maintained ever since.

The Appearance of Books and Compilations

Many scholars believe that classics and bibliographies emerged during the Xia Dynasty (2100–1600B.C.). This conclusion stems from multiple historical materials. *Shangshu*, the earliest history book found to date, says that records existed at the turn of the Xia and Shang. According to *Lüshi Chunqiu*,

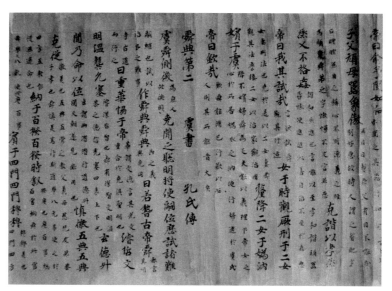

Shangshu from the Tang dynasty (618–907), the earliest Chinese history book that shows books were in existence during the Xia Dynasty.

another history book, during the Xia Dynasty there was not only a book ordinance but also an official Imperial Astronomer in charge of collecting and preserving books. *Lüshi Chunqiu* was once publicly displayed at the gate of Xianyang city for readers to edit. Gold rewards were promised to readers that could make improvements.

Certainly, the documents and records of the Xia Dynasty are simply written records, or documentary archive material, rather than formal books in the modern sense of the word. Nevertheless, they are carefully constructed records of people's activities. They have some merit as books.

During the Shang Dynasty, the ancient Chinese started writing on oracle bones, bronzes, jade, bamboo and wood to record information, which resulted in various types of document - oracle bone inscriptions, bronze epigraphs, jade, bamboo and wooden slips. In terms of content, form and distribution, these inscriptions have qualities and features similar to books. These inscriptions already show some elements of compilation through the process of writing, collecting and verifying, which can be regarded as the original editing activities before the emergence of formal books.

Governments started to establish special book collecting organizations during the Zhou Dynasty (1046–256 B.C.) when books truly emerged. After 770 B.C., feudal lords fought against one another while scholars gradually started writing more books.

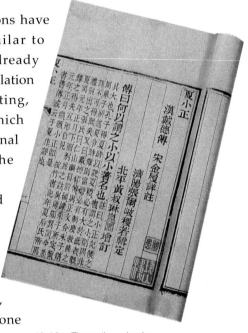

Xia Xiao Zheng, the calendar devised during the Xia Dynasty (2070–1600B.C.), still in use today, was recorded in this book.

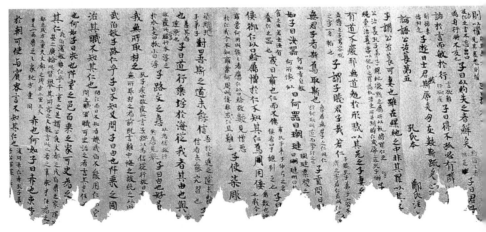

Surviving pages of the *Analects of Confucius* (Tang Dynasty version), which recorded Confucius' thoughts.

Confucius (551–479B.C.), the creator of Confucianism, edited and compiled many ancient classics and used them as textbooks in his teachings. Confucius might, therefore, be considered China's first well-known book editor.

From Oracle Bone to Paper: Media of Ancient Books

Pottery, bones, bronze, jade, bamboo and wood as well as silk were respectively used as materials on which to record Chinese characters in ancient times. After centuries of trial and error, papermaking was invented, which combined the merits of bamboo and wood slips with those of silk and overcame their deficiencies. Papermaking contributed tremendously to the history of publishing and indeed to the history of the world.

Oracle bones

The most common written records used by the ancient Chinese were oracle bones made of tortoise shell and animal bones, especially ox scapula. Characters carved on these became known as oracle bone inscriptions. As an important medium for Chinese characters throughout the Xia and Shang dynasties, oracle bone inscriptions were also very popular through the Yin, Shang and Western Zhou dynasties (1046–711 B.C.).

Most of the oracle bones that have been unearthed, mainly from the Yin ruins (Anyang city in Henan Province), are remnants from the mid- and late Shang Dynasty (1300–1046 B.C.). The Shang people were superstitious and sought the advice of deities and ancestors on any decision that needed to be made, whether about hunting, farming, astronomical phenomena, harvest, war, disease or sacrifices. As a result, most of oracle bones included

Oracle bone inscriptions on tortoise shell.

divination records from the time. In addition, there were a number of inscriptions recording important data such as numbers of prisoners of war, numbers of hunted animals, rewards and sacrifices. The records found on oracle bones touch upon various aspects of social life from ancient times.

Bronze wares

Inscriptions carved on bronze wares are called epigraphs or bronze inscriptions. During the Xia and Shang dynasties, a great number of bronze works were produced. The Western Zhou Dynasty (1600–771 B.C.) was the golden age of bronze.

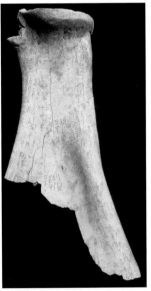

Oracle bones with inscriptions made up of relatively mature Chinese characters.

The "Great Ding" (tripod), made in the early Shang Dynasty, unearthed in Shang Cheng, Zhengzhou City.

With various styles and fine designs, bronze works can be classified as daily wares and musical instruments. When they started to be used as vessels in sacrificial ceremonies, bronze works became an authoritative emblem for building and consolidating state power. Due to such special recognition, the aristocracy would cast a piece of bronze and use it to inscribe important data or event records, all information that needed to be preserved for posterity.

To date, tens of thousands of inscriptions from the Shang to the Han Dynasty (206 B.C.–220 A.D.) have been found in China. A number are long

"Ligui" (a bronze altar made in the Western Zhou Period) bears the inscription of King Wu of Zhou, who annihilated the Shang Dynasty.

Bronze inscription on the Maogong Ding (tripod) and its rubbings.

passages, among which the longest is found on the Maogong Ding (tripod) with 497 words. The main contents of bronze inscriptions include records of sacrificial ceremonies, war, largess, government documents, emperors' speeches and tributes to ancestors. These are more abundant than oracle bone inscriptions.

Stone inscriptions

Ancient people used to carve chronicle scripts on stones that could be found more easily than metals and could be easily displayed.

The earliest stone inscriptions known in China are stone scripts in the shape of a drum dating to the Spring and Autumn Period (770–476 B.C.). Ten pieces of inscribed stones shaped like drums were unearthed in Fengxiang County, Shaanxi Province during the early Tang Dynasty. The inscribed characters

Stone drum and its rubbings.

Stone Classics of the Xiping Reign
The engraving of the Stone Classics of the Xiping Reign lasted nine years, from 175-183 AD, presided over by the noted scholar Cai Yong. There were forty-six stone monuments for seven Confucian classics: *I Ching, Poems of Lu State, The Book of Hisotry, The Srping and Autumn Annals, The Biography of Gongyang, Ceremonies and Rituals and Analects of Confucius.* The Stone Classics stood in front of the gate of the imperial college in Luoyang, the capital at the time, and attracted many visitors every day. As the earliest official definite edition of Confucian classics, the Stone Classics have an important place in the history of Chinese publishing.

are in a font somewhere between that used in bronze inscription and small official script and contain verses about hunting—they are called the "Hunting Tablets."

Emperor Qin Shihuang (259–210 B.C.) popularized stone inscriptions by using them in various places to publicize his efforts to unite the country as he undertook inspection tours throughout his twelve-year reign. During the Eastern Han Dynasty (25–220 A.D.), stone carvings became very popular. There were many great articles engraved on stone, among which the most famous was "Xiping Stone Classics." It launched the history of engraving ancient Confucian classics, playing a significant role in the development of books. Later generations followed suit and the result was a six-fold increase in inscribing activities. Of the resulting products, only the "Kaicheng Stone Classics of the Tang Dynasty" (now kept in the Forest of Steles in Xi'an) and the "Qianlong Stone Classics of the Qing Dynasty" (now kept in the Imperial Academy in Beijing) have been completely preserved.

Besides the Confucian classics, Buddhist and Taoist classics from various dynasties were also engraved on

stone. The most splendid were the Buddhist stone inscriptions at Mt. Shijing in Fangshan District, Beijing. A total of 3,572 volumes of 1,122 Buddhist classics were engraved on 14,278 stone sheets from the early seventh to the twelfth century. These stone inscriptions are called

The rubbings of Mt. Yi Stone Inscription by Qin Shihuang (the first emperor of the Qin Dynasty).

Kaicheng Stone Classics from the Tang dynasty (now kept in the Forest of Steles in Xiían).

"Tripitaka of Yunju Temple in Fangshan" or "Fangshan stone inscriptions."

Bamboo and wooden slips

Before the invention of papermaking, polished bamboo and wooden slips were the most widely used and the most influential writing materials. A single bamboo slip was called *Jian*, while numerous bamboo slips linked together were *Ce*, or *Jian Ce*. Blank wooden slips were called *Ban*, while written ones were *Du*. Slender wooden slips were called *Mu Jian* and linked wooden slips were *Ban Du*.

The use of bamboo and wood as writing materials can be traced back to the twenty-first century B.C. at least, even before

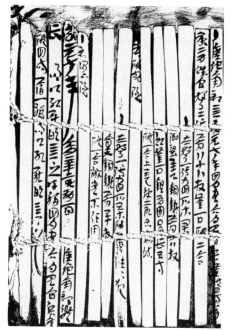
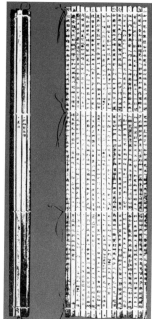

The thin wood script of weapons from the West Han Dynasty, unearthed in Juyan.

Wuwei bamboo and wood slips from the Han Dynasty.

the use of oracle bones, metal and stone.

In terms of content, bamboo and wooden slips can be classified into clerical documents and books which included Confucian classics, history and geography books, laws and regulations, military books and chronicles. Compared with oracle bones, stones and metal, bamboo and wood have their own merits. They are cheap and easy to produce. Moreover, the slips can be linked into volumes. As a result, along with silk and paper, bamboo and wood slips were used as writing material for hundreds of years, even after paper was invented. They did not cease to be viewed as useful writing materials until the end of the Eastern Jin Dynasty (317–420) in the fourth century.

Silk manuscripts

Silk manuscripts, or textile writing, are characters written on various kinds of silk, the production of which originated in China. According to ancient books, silk began to be used as a writing material no later than the Spring and Autumn Period and prevailed for about 700–800 years throughout the Warring States and Three Kingdoms Period (220–280).

One silk manuscript, unearthed in the Chu tomb of Changsha in 1934, is known as "the Chu Silk Manuscript." It includes written content about many important legendary figures surrounded by mysterious colored images in Chinese ink, drawn with writing brushes. This is the earliest silk manuscript found to date.

Many silk manuscripts were unearthed in the Mawangdui Han tombs in Changsha. In 1973, more than 120,000 words in twenty kinds of books were found, including *Laozi* (two versions), *I Ching, Intrigues of the Warring States* and *Strategies of the Warring States*. Silk was used not only in writing but also drawing, including diagrams and maps in bamboo and wooden slips. *Dao Yin Tu* and other ancient maps were discovered in the Mawangdui Silk Texts.

Part of "the Chu silk manuscripts" of the Warring States Period.

The merit of silk for writing is that it is not as heavy and clumsy as bamboo and wood slips, it can be easily cut into different sizes and was therefore convenient. It had a large capacity but required little space. However, due to its high cost, silk used in writing

Silk copy of the *Strategies of the Warring States.*

Version A and Version B of silk manuscripts of *Laozi*

was far beyond the reach of ordinary people. After years of exploration and practice, Chinese ancestors finally invented papermaking on the basis of silk-rinsing and retting techniques.

Papermaking technique

As one of the four great inventions of ancient China - along with printing, gunpowder and the compass - papermaking was a major achievement of ancient Chinese science and technology.

Numerous archeological findings show that the ancient Chinese invented plant fiber paper during the Western Han

Painting on silk from Tomb 1 of Mawangdui.

Dynasty based on long-term productive practice. Paper made during the Western Han Dynasty during every emperor's regime in the years' ranging from Wendi Emperor (180–157 B.C.) to the Xinmang Period (9–23 A.D.) has been unearthed. In 1986, ancient paper from 176–141 B.C., yellow, thin and soft, on which maps were drawn, was unearthed in the Fangmatan Han Tombs in Tianshui, Gansu Province. Gray and yellow paper with 50 words in 7 lines (written around 89–97 A.D.) was found in the Chake'ertie Hanfengsui Relic on the eastern bank of E'jina River, Gansu Province in 1942. Pale-yellow ancient paper, discovered in Tianshuijin Hanxuanquan Youyi Relic in Dunhuang, Gansu Province, was of refined texture with written words from around 8–23 A.D. The discovery of this large quantity of Western Han paper proves that plant fiber paper existed in China in the second century B.C.

The invention of plant fiber paper, which was convenient, inexpensive, light, soft and enduring, fundamentally changed the

Ancient paper with a map (from around 176–141 B.C. unearthed in Fangmatan, Gansu Province, 1986).

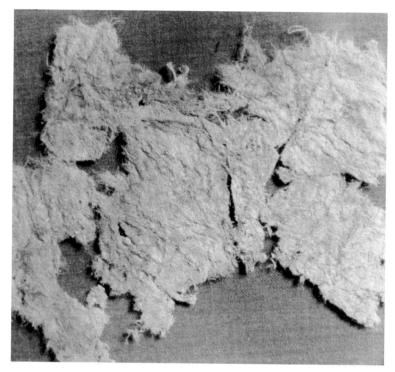

Pieces of ancient paper (unearthed in Majuanwan, Dunhuang, 1979).

media used to record and spread knowledge.

In 105 A.D., during the Eastern Han Dynasty, Cai Lun (c. 63–121 A.D.), having innovated papermaking, presented the emperor with paper he had made, earning high praise. From then on, this kind of paper grew in popularity across the country and became known as "Caihou Paper," named after the inventor. After this, paper, with gradually improving techniques and ever-lower costs, evolved as the most universal writing material. But not until the fourth century A.D. did paper replace bamboo, wood slips and silk and become the most popular writing material of society.

The restorative processes of papermaking. (No.1, 3: Washing. No. 2:
Cutting. No.4: Making plant ash water. No.5: Steaming and boiling. No.6: Ramming.
No.7: Routing. No.8: Paper making. No.9: Drying and releasing.)

The Evolution of Publishing

Marked with papermaking and printing techniques, the history of Chinese publishing can be divided into four stages: The bamboo inscription and silk manuscripts period from the establishment of Xia Dynasty (twenty-first century B.C.) to the second century B.C. (before the invention of papermaking); the manuscript book period from the first century B.C. to the seventh century A.D. (before the invention of printing); the manual printing period from the seventh century A.D. to the 1840s (before western printing machines came to China); and the mechanical printing period from 1840s to the early 1900s.

Since the twentieth century, Chinese publishing has officially entered the modern publishing era and has kept pace with the trends of global publishing.

Bamboo inscription and silk manuscripts (2100–200 B.C.)

During this period, Chinese publishing activities made rapid progress in the type of writing materials used, compiling, copying and forming.

In this period, the early evolution of Chinese characters, oracle bones, bronze inscriptions, seal scripts and clerical script improved the convenience of writing. Among the widely used writing materials, bamboo and wood were used across the country and resulted in an early book form of bamboo and wood slips.

The number and length of Chinese books increased as academic culture and the carriers of language developed. Books that could represent the essence of Chinese culture were written, such as the *Classic of Changes*, *The Book of Poetry*, *Analects of Confucius*, *Laozi*, *The Art of War of Sun Zi* and *Records of the Grand*

Relics of bamboo and wood slips from the Han Dynasty, found in Juyan, Gansu Province.

Historian. These, each thousands or tens of thousands words long, were written on bamboo and wood slips to hand down to later generations.

Book collection activities gradually expanded and the collection of books by government book agencies developed. Through a combination of compiling, arranging, writing and collecting, government book agencies began to act as government publishing agencies. A large quantity of government publications were published and distributed.

At the same time, academic development increased people's need for books. Confucian books were honored as the national classics of the Han Dynasty, which excited society's passion to pursue them. By means of transcription, borrowing and teaching, books became widespread.

Meanwhile, book transcribing became a special occupation and the trade evolved. With the bloom of the book business, Shusi, the earliest bookstore in Chinese history, came into being in the capital city of Chang'an and in other economically and culturally developed cities at the end of the second century B.C.

China had experienced economic and cultural communication with its neighboring countries since the third century B.C. At that time Buddhism was introduced into China and had a great influence on Chinese society.

Papermaking was invented in China in the second century B.C. After that, paper, as well as bamboo and wood slips, was used as writing material. Not until the early fifth century did paper, by order of the emperor, replace bamboo and wood slips and become popular.

Manuscript books (200 B.C.–700 A.D.)

It was in this period that the Chinese publishing industry experienced its early golden days. The initial stage of the manuscript book period lasted from the second century B.C.

to the fourth century A.D. During this stage, bamboo and wood slips, silk and paper were used as writing material in parallel. It flourished from the fifth to the seventh century A.D. After the eighth century, with the extensive application of printing, manuscript books co-existed with printed books for quite a long period before printed books became the mainstream. The history of manuscript books is more than one thousand years old.

After paper became popular thanks to constant improvements, a system of books, called a scroll system, was shaped from transcription to scroll making.

In that period, the number and variety of books increased significantly. Rough statistics suggest that about 11,754 works made up of 73,200 scrolls were produced from 25 A.D. to 618

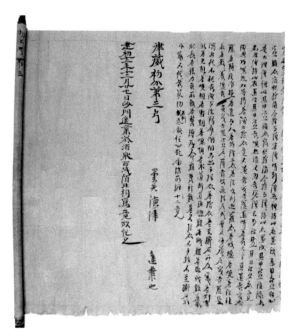

The 416 A.D. Buddhist Scriptures Manuscript. An early scroll found in the Dunhuang Grotto of Buddhist Texts, Gansu Province.

A.D, which included general encyclopedia, collected works, rhyme dictionaries, genealogies and other types of books. The translation of Buddhist scriptures boomed in this period and about 1,500 works on 4,000 strolls were translated from 220 A.D. to 618 A.D. At the same time, with the widespread use of paper, the number of words in a single work increased in quantity, and works with hundreds of thousands of words were quite common at the time.

With the increasing number and types of books, arranging and cataloguing emerged. During 26–6 B.C., Liu Xiang, with the emperor's support, organized scholars to create a systematic arrangement for the country's national book collection. With 13,269 books organized, it was the first large-scale book arrangement orchestrated by the state. In the process, Liu Xiang and others wrote a bibliography for each book and edited the first systematic book catalogue in ancient China.

The books were classified into six categories: "Six Classical Arts" referred to Confucianism classical works and reading materials for the "Six Meridians;" "The Philosophers" referred to selected readings of Confucian and other ancient Chinese classics since Pre-Qin Days; "Poetry" referred to Poems; "Han Odes" to literary output; "Military Book" to military works; "Shushu" and "Fangji" to works about natural and applied science. These are the well-known "Six Classifications" in Chinese history.

After this, there were efforts to arrange the national collection of books and the compilation of a library catalogue in each successive dynasty. Progress, however, led to great changes in the classification of books. In 636 A.D, *Sui Shu*, an official history book created by Wei Zheng and others included a "Bibliography of Chronicles" that recorded 3,127 collected books comprising of 36,708 chapters, and 1,064 lost books consisting of 12,759 chapters. Based on the previous book

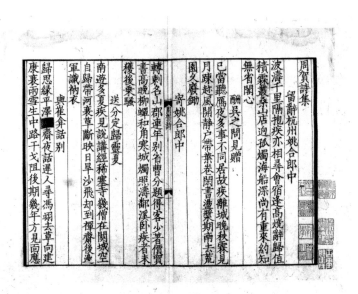

Zhou Heis Poems published by Chens Bookstore in Linían during the Southern Song Dynasty in Hangzhou, a representative product of workshop printing.

classification system, the recorded books were catalogued into four sections: *Jing, Shi, Zi* and *Ji*. "*Jing*" referred to Confucian classics works; "*Shi*" to various types of history books; "*Zi*" to readings of Confucian and other ancient Chinese classics as well as Buddhism, Taoism and other religious works; and "*Ji*" to literature works. This was the famous "Four Classifications" in ancient China, which had over forty minor catalogues. In addition, there were also Taoist scriptures and Buddhist scriptures attached.

The *Bibliography of Chronicles of the Sui Dynasty*, to a certain degree, reflects the profile and structure of Chinese books in the manuscript book period and the cultural features and structure of the traditional academy. It had a significant impact on book classification in later generations - library catalogues were established on this base. To this day, the "Four Classifications" is still employed in arranging and cataloguing ancient books in many places in China.

The major copying method in this period was transcription. As books became well known and people sought them out, the book trade became a growing business. There were numerous transcribers who earned their livelihoods by transcribing books. With the spread of papers and improvements in ink-making, unprecedented progress was made in duplicating techniques. Moreover, the invention of stamping and watercolor sealing techniques provided technical possibilities for the invention of printing techniques while traditional transcribing remained very popular.

Meanwhile, Chinese books and papermaking began to spread to Vietnam, Korea, Japan and other neighboring countries, greatly impacting the development of publishing there.

Manual printing (the seventh century A.D.–1840s)

From 700 to the 1840s, Chinese printing was stuck in block printing. The period is known as the "Manual Printing Period." The Chinese publishing industry reached its highest splendor during this period. Not later than the seventh century A.D, engraving, typography and registration printing were invented in China. These inventions marked a new stage in Chinese publishing that led to rapid progress in the quality and quantity of books. From then on, the Chinese publishing industry became increasingly more popular and soon developed into five systems, which were: government printing, private printing, workshop printing, temple printing and college printing. All these systems mutually influenced and stimulated one another in their development.

The government and private printing systems, with a rapid increase in the number of books published, entered an era of unprecedented prosperity. More than 14,000 works in 218,029 volumes were published during the Ming dynasty, some of

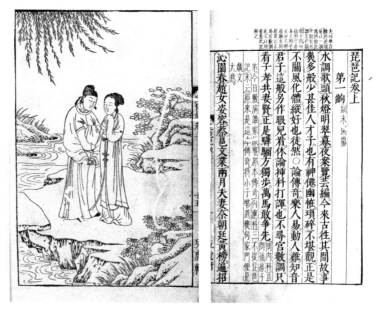

The 1597 version of *Story of Pipa* of the Ming Dynasty. At this time, reprints of dramas and novels were very popular.

which were huge classic works like the *Yongle Encyclopedia* and *Siku Quanshu*.

A large quantity of classics, like the Confucian classics, historical classics and the *Tripitaka*, were inscribed many times. Each copy represented a significant publishing event, which showed the publishing capability during the manual printing period of ancient China.

As production capacity grew, official and private book collections were enlarged and book collecting and preservation experience accumulated. There were many famous libraries like the Huang Shi Cheng Library and the Tian Yi Library. At the same time, not only government organizations and schools engaged in book publishing and selling, but civil book workshops began to do a more vigorous trade. In the big publishing centers around the country, there were countless book workshops. The

A carved copy of *the Original Meaning of I Ching of the Changes* of the Qing Dynasty from the inner court of the reign of Emperor Kangxi.

publishing industry, with new phenomenon like the emergence of book advertisements and copyright protection, developed as a commodity economy.

To meet the development needs of the printing industry, ancient Chinese books gradually evolved into album binding forms consisting of folding forms, butterfly-like binding, wrapped-ridge binding and thread binding, and finalized the design of thread-binding form.

In this period, book circulation and trade expanded and flourished further. Not only government organizations and schools engaged in book publishing and selling, but also civil book workshops undertook more vigorous trade. Exchanges of publications between China and foreign counties expanded so that lots of Chinese books were exported. Papermaking and printing spread across Asia and Europe. At the end of the sixteenth century, western missionaries started their translations and writings in China, which brought a new dimension to publishing and cultural circles.

However, in the nineteenth century, Chinese publishing still could not break away from manual printing and could not bring about capitalist management without a breakthrough in book content and format. As a result, Chinese publishing was left behind. After the Opium War in 1840, traditional Chinese society gradually collapsed and stepped towards modernization. With the introduction of modern Western publishing techniques, a fundamental revolution took place in Chinese publishing.

From this time on, Chinese publishing entered the machine-printing period. At the turn of twentieth century, many private publishing houses, like the Commercial Press and the Zhonghua Book Company, were established. China's publishing industry finally emerged from its backward condition and began to open a new chapter of modern publication.

Classical Ancient Books
The Workmanship of Ancient Chinese Books

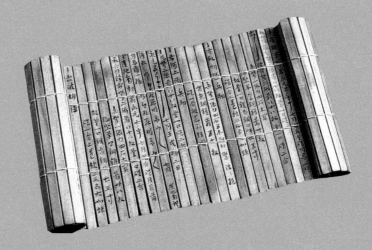

Selected Content of Ancient Books

In general, the editing format of ancient Chinese books can be divided into two kinds. One is the co-editing presided over by the government. Many books, such as *Yongle Encyclopedia*, *Siku Quanshu* and others were co-compiled in this way. The other is individual editing by an author or editor. Likewise, numerous books were individually-compiled, including *The Records of the Grand Historian, The Articles of the Whole Ancient Times, Three Generations, Qin and Han Dynasty, The Three Kingdoms and Six Dynasties* and others.

The content of ancient Chinese books is not only wide in scope but has also been continuously enriched and updated with the progress of time. The results are easily visible in the following statistical table for ancient Chinese works by Wang Yuguang.

Xueyan Study handwritten copy of *The Warring States Scheme* from the Ming Dynasty, which was arranged and named by Liu Xiang and others.

Table 1

Dynasty	Year	Total Number of Works	Total Volumes	Average Number of Works per Century	Growth Rate
West Han Dynasty and earlier (before 25 B.C.)	747	1033	13,029	138	
Eastern Han Dynasty (25-220)	195	1100	2900	564	309%
Wei, Jin, Southern and Northern and Sui Dynasties (220-618)	398	10,654	70,304	2679	375%
Tang and Five Dynasties (618-960)	342	10,806	185,074	3160	18%
Song Dynasty (960-1279)	319	11,519	124,919	3611	14%
Western Xia, Liao, Jian and Yuan Dynasties (906-1368)	462	5970	52,891	1292	-64%
Ming Dynasty (1368-1644)	276	14,024	218,029	5081	293%
Qing Dynasty (1644-1911)	295	126,649	1,700,000	42,932	745%
Republic of China before the Anti-Japanese War (1912-1937)	25	71,680	91,378	286,720	568%

Bibliographies of ancient Chinese books compiled by the past dynasties offer a sound reflection of the substance of the works.

Formal, large-scale proofreading and cataloguing in ancient China started during the Western Han Dynasty. At the end of the Western Han Dynasty, noted scholars Liu Xiang and Liu Xin (father and son) were tasked with systemizing the state book collection. The father and son team classified the books into six categories based on existing academic categories and bibliographies. The bibliography of *The Han Dynasty: Bolographic*

Treatise roughly illustrates the classifications the father and son used. It is outlined below.

Outline—Preface

Six classical arts—nine types, namely, *Yi, Shu, Shi, Li, Yue, Chunqiu, Lunyu, Xiaojing* and *Xiaoxue*; recorded books by 129 scholars, 2,926 articles and one picture scroll.

Various Schools of Thought and their exponents—ten types, namely, Confucian, Dao, Yinyang, Fa, Ming, Mencius, Zongheng, Za, Nong and Xiaoshuo; recorded books by 187 scholars, 4,346 articles.

Poems—20 Quyuan-like scholars, 21 Lujia-like scholars, 25 Sunqing-like scholars, 5 types of Za Fu and Sing poetry; recorded books by 106 scholars, 1,313 articles.

Military—4 types of *Quanmou, Xingshi, Yinyang* and *Jiqiao*; recorded books by 66 scholars, 1,375 articles, 44 scrolls of pictures.

Mathematics—6 types of astronomy, *Lipu, Wuxing, Zhugui, Zazhan* and *Xingfa*; recorded books by 110 scholars, 2,557 articles.

Science—4 types of *Yijing, Jingfang, Fangzhong* and *Shenxian*; recorded books by 36 scholars, 862 articles.

In total, there were records for 13,397 books in 38 types and 6 categories, written by 634 scholars with 45 scrolls of pictures.

The *Six Classical Arts* refers to Confucian classic works and basic readings on the "six meridians." Among the most significant are "Paying Supreme Tribute to Confucianism" in the Han Dynasty, "The Philosophers outside the Confucians," the selected readings of Confucius and other ancient Chinese classics

Portrait of Ji Yun, chief-editor of *Siku Quanshu*.

in pre-Qin Days. "Sing poetry" refers a popular style of poetry during the Han Dynasty, which led to it being singled out as a specific category. "Military" works, which were very effective in consolidating the feudal regime an age of frequent war, were many in the Spring and Autumn and Warring States Periods," so they ranked above "Mathematics" and "Science." The "Mathematics" and "Science" categories mainly refer to the works about natural and applied science. "Outline" means "the compendium of six categories" or "the compendium of all books," which explains the significance of the six categories and their academic origins and elaborates on the interrelation and application of the six categories.

After the Han Dynasty, book classification changed according to the development of China's publishing industry. In the early Tang Dynasty, the *Bibliography of Chronicles of the Sui Dynasty*, by Wei Zheng (580–643) and others, adopted the "Four Classifications" of "*Jing, Shi, Zi* and *Ji*" with a supplement containing Taoist scriptures and Buddhist scriptures. In addition, there were 40 minor-catalogues below the Four Categories: 10 "*Jing*" catalogues, 13 "*Shi*" catalogues, 14 "*Zi*" catalogues, 3 "*Ji*" catalogues, 4 "*Tao*" and 11 "*Buddha*" catalogues. Their specific lists were as follows:

"*Jing*": *Yi, Shu, Shi, Li, Yue, Chunqiu, Lunyu, Xiaojing, Chenwei Shu* and *Xiaoxue*

"*Shi*": *Zhengshi, Gushi, Zashi, Bashi, Qijuzhu, Jiushi, Zhiguan, Yizhu, Xingfa, Zazhuan, Dili, Puxi* and *Bulu*.

"*Zi*": *Confucianism, Dao, Fa, Ming, Mo, Zongheng, Za, Nong, Xiaoshuo, Bing*, astronomy, *Lisu, Wuxing*, and *Yifang*.

"*Ji*": *Chuci, Bieji* and *Zongji*.

"Supplement": Taoist scriptures and Buddhist scriptures.

The book classifications offer a rough reflection of book publication and academic development before the Tang Dynasty. The "Four Classifications" system in *Bibliography of Chronicles of the Sui Dynasty* exerted a tremendous influence on later book categories, typified by the most comprehensive, abundant and influential *General Catalogue of Four Treasuries.*

The *General Catalogue of Siku Quanshus,* also called the *General Index of the Complete Works of the Siku Quanshu,* was linked to the compiling of *Siku Quanshu* during the Qing Dynasty. This is the summary of the works, written by the editors, finalized by the chief editor Jiyun (who also called himself Xiaolan, 1724–1805) and authorized by the Emperor, to include the content, the dynasty of writing, the writer's biography and the original version of the book. The book records 3,461 kinds of ancient works in 79,309 volumes in *Siku Quanshu,* and 6,793 kinds in 93,550 volumes not included in *Siku Quanshu,* which basically includes ancient Chinese works before the Period of Emperor Qianlong of the Qing Dynasty. With 200 volumes, the book can be divided into 4 classifications, 44 categories and 66 minor-catalogues.

"Jing": *Yi, Shu, Shi, Li, Chunqiu, Xiaojing, Wujing, Sishu, Yue* and *Xiaoxue* in 10 minor-catalogues.

"Shi": *Zhengshi, Biannianshi, Jishibenmoshi, Zashi, Bieshi, Zhaolingzhouyi, Zhuanji, Shichao, Zaiji, Shiling, Dili, Zhiguan, Zhengshu, Mulu* and *Shiping* in 15 minor-catalogues.

"Zi": Confucianism, *Bingjia, Fajia, Nongjia, Shijia,* astronomy, *Shushu, Yishu, Pulu, Zajia, Leishu, Xiaoshuojia, Yijia* and *Daojia* in 14 minor-catalogues.

"Ji": *Chuci, Bieji, Zongji, Shiwenping* and *Ciqu* in 5 minor-catalogues.

The *General Catalogue of Siku Quanshu,* featuring a complete collection of traditional book-cataloguing with a total order for each category, a short preface for each catalogue and an abstract for each book, is an agglomeration of the Four Classifications in ancient books. It is a summary of the academy in China before the eighteenth century and has great academic value.

Printing and Transcription: Reproduction of Ancient Publications

The invention of movable-type print is a significant event in the development of human society. Printing techniques in ancient China included three distinct types: block-printing, movable-type printing and registration printing, of which block-printing was the earliest and most popular. Following the invention of movable-type printing, China's printing industry bloomed but the tradition of transcription remained, giving the new period of printing a traditional flavor.

Engraving printing

Engraving printing was also called whole-page printing or block printing. Pear wood or Chinese jujube tree wood was usually used to make a block, and then thin paper with characters written in reverse (a mirror-image) was stuck on the surface of the block and engraved into the wood. Then it was only necessary to ink the base slab and bring it into contact with the paper or cloth to achieve an acceptable print. In ancient times, this technique was called woodblock printing because people pressed the paper on the surface of the prepared and inked woodblock. Based on current evidence, it seems that printing techniques were invented in China no later than between the seventh

Tools used in engraving printing.

and the eighth century (during the early and glorious period of the Tang Dynasty), and most likely at the turn of the seventh century A.D.

In surviving documents from the Tang Dynasty, there are many records that describe the invention and the application of printing during the Tang Dynasty. In the preface of Bai Juyi's (779–831) *Chang Qing Collection* 《长庆集》, in the fourth year of Emperor Tang Mu, the poet Yuan Zhen wrote that Bai Juyi and Yuan Zhen's poems were published in quantities, sold in bookstores and widely read. In 835, the government banned private printing because private publishing workshops had printed a huge number of calendars. All this suggests that block printing was widely used in the ninth century, so it is possible to infer that block printing was invented earlier.

All existing early prints were made during the Tang Dynasty. The two best-known examples are the *Diamond Sutra,* unearthed in Dunhuang, China in 868. This is the earliest wood block print in existence. The *Diamond Sutra* is a complete scroll with

The printed copy of *Diamond Sutra* from the Tang Dynasty, 868.

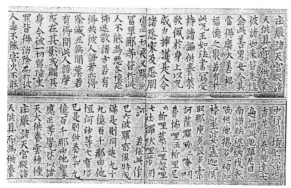

Pure Light Dharani Sutra unearthed in South Korea.

simple but heavy-colored illustrations, delicate painting, skilled cutting, and even ink printing. It was made with a mature technique and was definitely not the output of early stage printing.

The other is the Chinese character print from Empress Wu Zetian's period (690–705) of the Tang Dynasty. This was

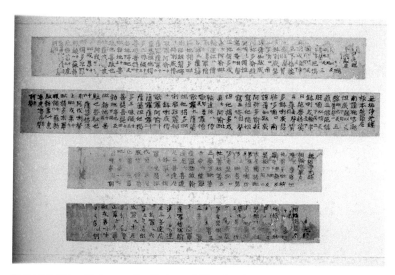

Pure Light Dharani Sutra unearthed in Japan (Million Sutra).

unearthed from Korea and Japan in the twentieth century. It includes the *Pure Light Dharani Sutra* unearthed in the Sarira pagoda in the Pulguksa Temple, Gyeongju, Korea and the Million Sutra made before 770 A.D. under the command of Empress Shotoku. It is kept in Horyuji in Yamatoji, Japan and the British Museum.

These findings in Korea and Japan show that Chinese woodblock printing developed at a relatively higher level and that the quality and scale was good enough for international export.

Movable-type printing

Movable-type printing is a system of printing and typography that uses movable components to reproduce the elements of a document (usually individual characters or punctuation) by making up single tablets in lines. Tablets can be separated after use and rearranged for another printing.

Bi Sheng (?–1051) invented ceramic movable type, the earliest movable type known, during the Northern Song Dynasty (960–1127). The invention is described in detail in *Dream Pool Essays* 《梦溪笔谈》 by Shen Kuo (1031–1095), from which we learn about the process of movable-type printing.

After Bi Sheng's death, movable type was continued by Shen Kuo's later generations, and was still used when the book *Dream Pool Essays* was written. This proves the reliability and authority of the book. Afterwards, Bi Sheng's

Portrait of Bi Sheng.

The restored graph of the wheel of the composing frame invented by Wang Zhen.

successors continued to use movable-type printing in later generations.

During the early Yuan Dynasty (1206–1368), the agronomist Wang Zhen made significant innovations in wooden movable-type printing. In 1298, Wang Zhen applied wooden movable-type printing to produce 100 copies of the *Records of Jingde County* in a single month by himself. The *Records of Jingde County* has more than sixty-thousand words. In addition, Wang wrote about his experience in an article named *Ways to Make Types and Print Books* to preserve the process. He also invented the wheel of the composing frame with movable-type characters arranged primarily through a rhyming scheme. Workers could pick up tablets by rotating the wheel while sitting.

Wooden movable-type printing spread to minority group areas and was used to print their books during the Yuan dynasty. Hundreds of wooden movable types in the Uighur language were found in Buddhist caves in Dunhuang, Gansu Province.

The printing of *Wu Ying Dian Ju Zhen Ban Collections* in 1773, with 134 kinds in more than 2,300 volumes, was the largest scale wooden movable-type printing effort of the Qing Dynasty.

The wooden movable type with Uighur script, the earliest alphabetic writing from the early thirteenth century, unearthed in Dunhuang caves.

Jin Jian, who took charge of the edition, recorded his printing experience in *Wu Ying Dian Selective Collections*, which was an important record of China's publishing history and has been translated into German, English and other languages.

Ancient Chinese metal movable type included bronze, tin and lead type, in which handmade bronze type was used first and

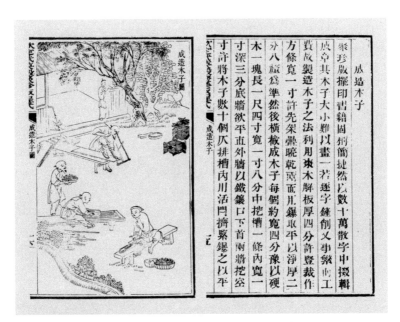

The illustration of Working Processes from *Wu Ying Dian Selective Collections*, a wooden movable type copy from the Qianlong period of the Qing Dynasty.

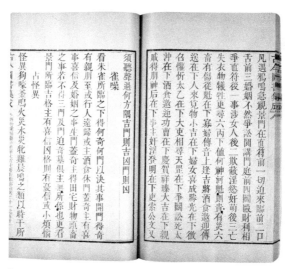

A copy printed with bronze movable-type of *The Compendium of Works of Past and Present* from the Qing Dynasty.

most often. Bronze type printing flourished at the end of fifteenth century. The best-known examples come from rich families known as Huasui, Huajian and Anguo, who printed books with bronze type in Wuxi of Jiangsu.

The most famous bronze movable-type print was the inner court of *The Compendium of Works of Past and Present* in Qing Dynasty. From the fourth to sixth year of the Yongzheng Period (1726–1728), the Qing government printed 65 copies comprised of 5,200 volumes, each in large and small fonts. This was an unprecedented printing effort with exquisite typography.

Color woodcut printing

Color woodcut printing was based on woodblock printing, which can successively print several colors on the same piece of paper by using different sizes of blocks with different colors. Books printed with this technique are called registration editions.

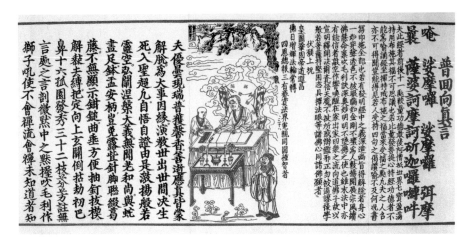

Notes to Wuwen Monk Diamond Sutra carved by Zifu Temple in the early years of the Yuan Dynasty (1340).

Early in the use of this technique, the most common colors used were red and black—these books are called "Prints in red and black" or "Mackle prints." Later, the overprinted books became known as "Four-color prints" or "Five-color prints" according to the number of colors involved.

Based on archeological discoveries, it seems that color woodcut printing was invented, closely following the invention of xylography, during the period of the Song, Liao and Jin dynasties (960–1234). Three color overprinted "Nama Sakyamuni Buddha" survive, estimated to date from the Tonghe Period of the Liao Dynasty (982–1012), found in Fougong Temple,

Min's version of three-color overprint of *Notes and Commentary of the Three Classics* from the Wanli Period of the Ming Dynasty.

The four-color overprint of the *Guwen Yuanjian* in the Kangxi Period of the Qing Dynasty.

Yu Tang Fu Gui, the Suzhou Taohuawu New-Year picture, from the Qing Dynasty, printed with color woodcut printing techniques.

Yingxian County, Shanxi Province. The *Notes to Wuwen Monk Diamond Sutra* engraved in 1340 with two colors also survives: red as the text and black as notes, as well as red-black illustrations at the front of the book. Their existence suggests that color woodcut printing was already used in book printing during this period.

In the late Ming Dynasty (sixteenth-seventeenth century), color woodcut printing became popular. Surviving books of this kind are mostly the outputs from the families of Min Qiji and Ling Mengchu in Wuxing (today's Zhejiang province) during the Wanli period (1563–1620) of the Ming Dynasty. According to rough statistics, the two families printed 145 kinds of books, 13 of which are three-color prints, four are four-color prints and one is a five-color version. The two families, engaged in the same business for generations, are legendary in Chinese printing history.

Color woodcut printing was further developed during the

Qing Dynasty. According to *Aggregation of the Carvings in China*, there were more than forty multi-color block print shops during the Qing Dynasty. The representative overprints at the time are the official versions of the four-color *Guwen Yuanjian*, the two-color *Anthology Selected by Emperors* in the Kangxi period, the four-color *Imperial Tang and Song Collection* as well as the five-color *Chuang-Sian-Jing-Kur* from the Qianlong reign. Private printing also yielded good works, such as two popular versions of *Du Gongbu Collection* in the Daoguang Period (1820–1850). One was Lukun's six-color version in Zhuozhou, and the other was Ye Yun'an's five-color version in Guangdong.

Common Development and Prosperity—Five Major Publishing Systems

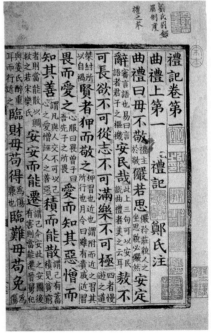

Ancient Chinese printing was the most advanced in the world. The foundations of three publishing systems—government, private and bookshop—were settled as early as the Tang and Five Dynasties Period. Besides these three, there were two other quite influential systems: temple and book institutes. Together, they created a unique publishing system. In long-term development, each system contributed to ancient printing and played a part in the spread and preservation of ancient books, culture and knowledge.

Annotations of the Book of Rites printed by Fuzhou Gongshiku in 1177.

Official printing: government publishing

Official printing refers to the publishing sector funded or hosted by central governmental institutions or local cultural or administrative organizations. Before the invention of printing, governments of many periods were involved in the continuous collection, editing, transcribing and dissemination of books and records. But because of the low efficiency of the transcription process, which was the main method of reproduction, the scale of publication was also constrained. It was the government's realization of the advantages of printing technology that led to large-scale printing of books. Gradually, an influential official printing system emerged.

Printing by the government was started by Feng Dao during the Five Dynasties period. It became prosperous throughout the Song and Yuan dynasties and reached its heyday during the Ming and Qing dynasties. Official printing generally consisted of central and local government printing: the Imperial College in the Song Dynasty, the Central Inner Court in the Ming Dynasty and the Wuyingdian in the Qing Dynasty were

Feng Dao and the first printing of Confucian classics
Inspired by popular non-official publishing and to help the public benefit from Confucian classics, Feng Dao (882–954), a prime minister during the Five Dynasties, made a request to the emperor in the third year of Changxing of the later Tang Dynasty (932AD) to have the nine Confucian classics printed based on the Kaicheng Stone Classics. The nine were *I Ching*, *Book of Odes*, *The Book of History*, *Rites of the Zhou*, *The Book of Rites*, *Etiquette and Ceremonies*, *The Zuo Commentary of the Spring and Autumn Annals* and *The Gongyang Commentary* and *The Guliang Commentary*. His request was granted and printing commenced in that year, but was not completed until 935. Besides the nine classics, another three books were also printed: *The Annotation of Classics, Classical Characters and Jiujing Ziyang*. Since this project was supervised by the imperial academy, these books are known as the "Jianben version of the nine Confucian classics in the Five Dynasties period." They heralded official book printing in China and had far-reaching impact on the dynasties that followed. For example, the imperial academy during the Song Dynasty used these books as the basis for their reproductions of the work. Feng Dao is regarded as the founder of the official printing and publishing of Confucian classics in Chinese history.

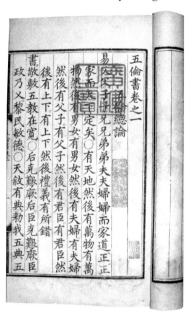

Jingchang edition of *Wulunshu* printed during the Zhengtong period of the Ming Dynasty (1436–1450).

The imperial court copperplate print of *Plowing and Weaving* from the reign of Emperor Kangxi of the Qing Dynasty.

the important institutions of central government printing in their respective times. Gongshiku Printing in the Song Dynasty and Seignior Printing were the representatives of local government printing.

After the Opium War, official printing declined and was gradually replaced by modern publishing. Since its inception, government book printing followed a distinct path, to serve as a tool to influence the public and to maintain feudal rule. The content was focused on Confucian classics, historical records and compilations driven by emperors. With strong financial support and talented workers, the quality of books from this system was guaranteed and served as a model for the whole publishing industry. This sector was also a major contributor to the preservation of ancient classics, the popularization of knowledge and enhancements in the quality of books.

Bookshop printing: non-official publishing

Shufang (bookshops), also called *Shulin, Shupu, Shutang* or *Shupeng*, evolved from the *Shusi* of the Han Dynasty. Their predecessors are book stands on the street and the book vendors

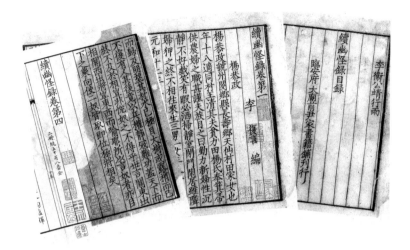

Xuyou Guailu printed by Yin's bookshop of Lin'an in the Song Dynasty.

who sold books to pedestrians. After the invention of printing, the business scope of bookshops expanded from retail and wholesale to compiling, editing, writing, carving and printing. In essence, they combined the functions of a publishing house, printing workshop and bookstore. Books from this source were oriented towards the general public and their ultimate purpose was profit. This type of publishing was more commercial than official and private publishing and is similar to today's private publications.

In the ancient Chinese book-printing system, bookshops became numerous during the Tang Dynasty. They were the major force for the production of ancient books and also the mainstream of commercial book circulation. They adopted block printing first, which laid the foundation for the rise of official and private book printing. Over a thousand years, many famous book-printing families emerged, who took great pains to build their businesses, handed down from generation to generation, and enjoyed a lasting significance. Thereby, they contributed to the spread and preservation of traditional culture. Of the many famous printing families, the most well known are the Yu of Jian'an and Chen of Lin'an during the Song and Yuan dynasties.

Private Printing: Personal Publishing

Private printing refers to privately funded book printing. Most ancient private book printing families were senior officials, rich businessmen or scholars who put a heavy emphasis on the quality of books. Their books are characterized more by the idea of "working for reputation" and less for business interests.

Many private book publishers were well-known academics. They combined book printing and studies. In the process of collecting, editing and printing, they also conducted proofreading, critical interpretation, textual research, literature studies and directory compilation and built up and enriched the "Theory of Compiling Books." Some private printers also made bold technical innovations, such as the development of copper type, registration, assembled block printing, blind embossing, and the employment of facsimile printing and other techniques to restore and preserve the appearance of ancient editions. Therefore, many private printed books are of high quality.

Ancient Chinese private book printing began during the Tang Dynasty. It was

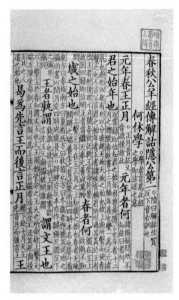

Kung-Yang's Commentary on the Spring and Autumn Annals printed by Wanjuantang of Yu Renzhong in 1191.

The private edition of the *Collection of Changli* by Liao Yingzhong from the Xianchun period of the Song Dynasty (1265–1274).

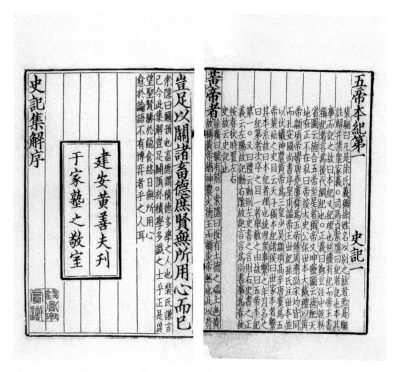

Home-school edition of Huang Shanfu's *Annotation to the Record of Grand Historians* from Jianían, Song Dynasty.

popular during the Song Dynasty with an output famous for high-quality classic and historical works as well as collections of poems and articles by celebrities.

In the late Ming Dynasty, private printing was more active with the emergence of a group of known private publishers, of whom Mao Jin was the most famous. Mao Jin (1599–1659) was born in Changshu, Jiangsu Province. He was engaged in private printing from around his thirties and built "Jiguge" and "Mugenglou," with a collection of over 80,000 books. Throughout his life, he had high-quality versions of his collection printed. With over 600 books and more than 100,000 blocks used, it made him the most

A picture of Jiguge of Mao Jin in Yushan

productive private publisher in China.

Generally, private printing during the Qing Dynasty fell into two categories. One was writings of past scholars and works by the printer. In most cases, with types based on handwriting as well as selected ink and paper, most of the books from this source were refined products. The other category was book series, lost books and old editions printed by book collectors and experts engaged in the restoration of ancient books after the rise of the "Theory of Textual Criticism."

College printing: academic publishing

College education represented a unique culture and educational base during the Tang and Song dynasties (618–1279). Originating in the Tang Dynasty, it became popular during the Northern Song and reached its peak in the Southern Song. It continued to the end of the Qing Dynasty. According to statistics, there were more than 6,600 colleges throughout the history of China. In these colleges, besides lecturing, teaching, writing and

Mao's Jiguge edition of *Zhongwu Jiwen* in the late Ming Dynasty.

academic research, editing and publishing were also regular activities. The result was the formation of the college printing system.

The Song and Yuan dynasties (960–1368) witnessed a boom in college printing. With ample income and capital and also well-known scholars, printing in colleges flourished and produced many good publications. The typical example is *Comprehensive Studies in Administration* by Hangzhou West Lake College in the first year of Taiding (1324). During the Ming and Qing dynasties (1368–1911), publishing by colleges was further strengthened and large-scale printing became common. The number of books printed by colleges in the Qing Dynasty topped the number from any other period.

The official and private operation of colleges ensured that their publications covered a wide array of topics, including "Jing," "Shi," "Zi" and "Ji." At the same time, they were student-centered, so the focus was academic publication, particularly the inheritance from certain schools. College editions can be divided into three types: writing and research notes of teachers and students for academic research, reference works and works by successive masters and famous writings to spread academic ideas and theories. With an emphasis on academia and supported by abundant funds, college editions are often highly refined.

Temple and monastery publications: religious publishing

Temple printing refers to the publishing of religious classics by temples. These books are called *"Focang"* or *"Daozang"* (Taoist canon). They are similar to today's religious publications. Their

Gate of Yuelu College in Changsha City of Hunan Province

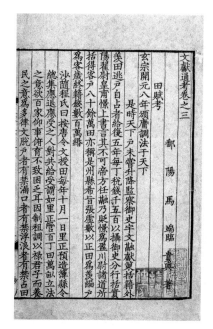

Hangzhou West Lake College printed edition of *Comprehensive Studies in Administration* from the Taiding Period (1324–1328) of the Yuan Dynasty.

efforts were supported by governments and Buddhist and Taoist classics were popular. These two factors helped give rise to an independent publishing system.

The most primary outputs of Buddhist temple print shops during the 800 years from the Song to the Qing Dynasty were the seventeen Chinese *Tripitakas* and a number of *Tripitakas* in minority languages (including Tangut, Mongolian, Tibetan and Manchu). Among all the *Tripitikas*, *The Northern Song Dynasty Official Version of the Tripitaka* (also known as *"Kaibaozang"*) printed in the Kaibao period (968–976) of the Song Dynasty was the first printed *Tripitaka* in the world.

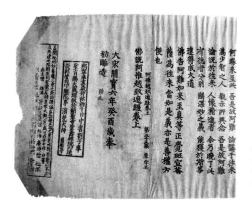

An incomplete page of *Kaibaozang*, printed with government funding in the early Northern Song Dynasty.

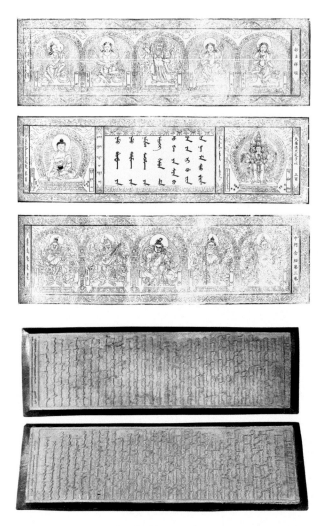

Tripitaka

The so-called *Tripitaka* are Buddhist canons of scriptures which comprise a huge collection of all the Buddhist classics organized in a systematic manner. Therein, the first category, the "Vinaya Pitaka," is the code of ethics. The second category, the "Sutra Pitaka" consists primarily of accounts of the Buddha's teachings. The third category is the "Abhidharma Pitaka." *Tripitaka* is also known as "*Sanzangjing*" or "*Yiqiejing*." "*Zang*" in Sanskrit is Pitaka, and it initially referred to a bamboo basket, containing the meaning of the collection. The *Tripitaka* is always very extensive, usually over 5,000 volumes. With as many as over 100,000 type plates, thousands of people were involved in writing, proofreading, type carving, printing and circulation. It took more than 10 years - and sometimes several decades or a century - to complete the work.

The two red-color printed pictures of *Tripitaka* and type plate in Manzhu language, the printing started in 1773 and took seventeen years to complete.

Taoism is a native religion in China. With specific compilation efforts, collections and organizational structure, *Daozang* is a large series of Taoist classics. In addition, the book also contains hundreds of schools of thought and many ancient works of

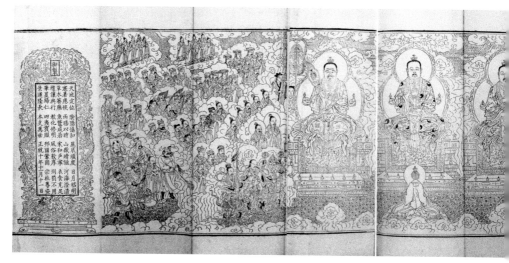

The excerpt of *Selection of Daozang* printed in 1445.

science and technology, including medicine, health, alchemy, astronomy, astrology and other topics.

Compilation of *Daozang* began during the Northern Zhou Dynasty (557–581). During the Zhenghe period of the Song Dynasty (1111–1118), the first printed version of Daozang, *Wanshou Daozang*, whose printing was presided over by the emperor, came out in 5,481 volumes. It was distributed to temples across the nation. With a total of 5,305 volumes, the extant copies of ancient China's *Daozang* are "the orthodox *Daozang*" printed in the Ming Dynasty (1445).

From Bamboo Strips to Stitched Binding: The Ancient Art of Bookbinding and Layout

Taking the invention of papermaking and printing as the demarcation point, the history of books in China can be divided into three phases with a corresponding book system. Bamboo strips and silk manuscripts coexisted before the invention of paper during the Han Dynasty. Scroll roll binding in the paper book period existed between the Han and Tang dynasties. And the album leaf system popular in the era of printed text prevailed after the invention of printing in the Tang Dynasty. Obviously there was some overlap between these systems.

Jiandu (bamboo and wooden strips)

Before the invention of paper, most Chinese books were written on bamboo or wooden strips. One bamboo strip was called "Jian," and many of them were bound to form a complete document which was known as "Ce." "Jian" and "Ce" were called "Jiance." Processed wooden strips with no characters written on them were called "Ban." Those with characters were called "Du" and thin ones were named "Mujian."

Books made of wooden strips were called "Bandu." For the convenience of reading and collecting, many "Jian" were bound with hemp fiber or hide rope. Bound "Jian" could be folded with the last piece as the scroll, making a volume of a book which could be unfolded from the first piece while reading. This was

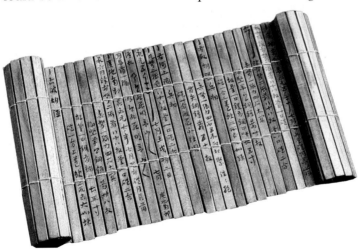

The restoration of Jiandu made of bamboo and wooden strips.

known as the Jiandu system, which was the earliest form of bookbinding and was used for thousands of years.

In the fifth century, with the wide application of paper and the appearance of paper texts, Jiandu was replaced.

The Scroll System

The scroll system evolved from the volume system and took its final shape during the time of silk manuscripts. It was used in the era of paper texts and a complete system was formed that is still used to mount books or paintings in modern China.

The procedure was as follows. A piece of wood working as a scroll was stuck on the end of the paper roll, and papers were rolled onto the scroll. Characters written directly onto silk sheets or, in the case of paper texts, pieces of paper with characters, were stuck onto the scroll in the correct order. A piece of paper

The scroll edition of *Qimin Yaoshu.*

or silk with no characters was named "Piao." Solid and resilient, it was attached to the beginning of the books with a scroll roll for the purpose of protection. A string was tied to the top of the "Piao" to bind the scroll. To mark the content of the books and make retrieval easier, a small tablet called "Qian" was often hung on the scroll and some were attached on the end of string, which was fixed after binding.

While reading, the scroll was open and unfolded. After reading, the scroll was rolled, tied by a string and placed flat with one end of the scroll facing the outside on a bookshelf. Readers could just take them out as needed and insert them back on the shelf later. This system was called "Chajia."

Transition from scroll to album leaf

Accordion binding

Palm sutras in "fanjiazhuang" were introduced from India to China from the seventh to ninth century and gave Chinese scholars inspiration. Rather than folding a long roll, they could be folded back and forth in a rectangular shape. A hard board was used at the front and back to protect the folds in a concertina

A carved copy of *Manchu Tripitaka* in Fanjiazhuang from 1736–1795.

Different kinds of concertina bound books collected in the National Palace Museum.

binding. These scrolls folded into concertina eliminated the need to unroll half a scroll to see a passage in the middle.

Whirlwind binding

Whirlwind binding evolved from scroll rolls. It is shaped like a scroll and based on a long paper on which the first page is stuck. The second page is stuck on the base with a paper strip on the right side with no characters, and other pages are stuck under

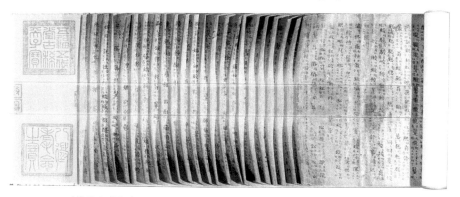

Whirlwind binding edition of *Wang Renxuis Kanmiu Buque Qieyun*, the only extant whirlwind binding example from the Tang Dynasty.

the last page from the left side. With pages collected together, the whirlwind binding edition of a book is read from the right side to the left side page after page, and is rolled from the end of the book.

This binding method was called "whirlwind binding" because of the circular movement of the page, which is like a whirlwind. When the book is unfolded, pages are arranged like dragon's scales. Therefore, it is also known as "dragon's scale" binding. *Wang Renxu's Kanmiu Buque Qieyun*, a manuscript from the Tang Dynasty collected in the National Palace Museum is a representative of whirlwind binding.

Album leaf

From the late Tang to the early Song, printed books gradually replaced manuscripts, and album leaf replaced the scroll system.

Album leaf refers to binding several single leaves into a volume suitable for printing. The earliest album leaf system was butterfly binding, which evolved into wrapped-back binding and then stitched binding. When machine-based printing was introduced, binding gradually moved to paper and hard-cover binding.

Butterfly binding

The name butterfly binding emerged from its resemblance to a butterfly when the book was spread out. It was the main layout system used during the Song Dynasty. In butterfly binding, two pages were printed on a sheet, which was then folded inwards. The sheets were pasted

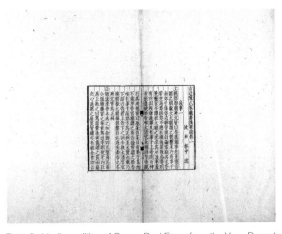

Butterfly-binding edition of *Dream Pool Essay* from the Yuan Dynasty.

together at the fold to make a codex with alternate openings of printed and blank pairs of pages. A hard cover (sometimes coated with cloth or silk) was made. In appearance, it looked like a modern paper or hardcover bound book and the shape of the leaves and the manner in which the book opened and closed resembled the wings of a butterfly.

Wrapped-back binding

In wrapped-back binding, pages are folded the opposite way round. Each sheet of paper was only printed on one side but, after folding, the woodblock print would appear on the "outside" rather than the "inside" of the folio. These folios were then piled up on top of each other so that the open ends, instead of the

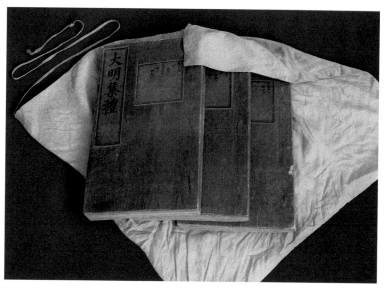

The wrapped-back-binding version of *Daming Jili*, from the Ming Dynasty.

edges, came together to form the spine. Wrapped-back binding appeared during the late Southern Song dynasty and remained in practice after the sixteenth century. The famous *Yongle Encyclopedia* is an example of a wrapped-back edition.

Stitched-bound books from the Qing Dynasty.

Stitched binding

Stitched binding first appeared in the sixteenth century. It developed from wrapped-back binding. The woodblock print would appear on the "outside" rather than the "inside" of the folio. Each group was made up of two or more sheets of paper joined together with thread at the fold. The spines of each of the gatherings are sewn together and then brought together to form the book.

Usually four holes were made on a stitched-bound book and such editions were called "four-needle-eye editions." For larger books, two more holes were punctured. These were called "six-needle-eye editions." Sometimes thread or silk were used to bind the two corners up and down to protect the books and make them look nice. Such books were called "corner-wrapped editions." Another kind of stitched book was called "rough editions" because the pages were not cut to be identical in size after the holes were made. Stitched books are easy to read, durable and practical. This type of binding is still used today for copies of ancient books using deckle-edged paper or rice paper, which gives them a simple and elegant look.

The appearance of stitch binding represents the last phase in the history of traditional Chinese bookbinding. After the eighteenth century, machine-based printing gradually adopted the appearance of paperback and hardcover books.

Layout of printed edition

All woodblock printed books are printed on one side of the page only and each page has a certain format. Usually a single page format includes layout, boundary box, boundary line, core, fish tail, trunk, head, foot, ear and so on.

Typeface: The area of one type.

Type frame: Black lines around a typeface are also called boundary lines. A single line frame is called a single boundary line while a double line frame was called double line boundary.

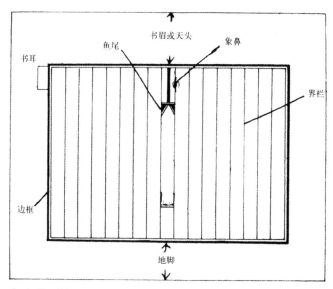

Ancient book layout.

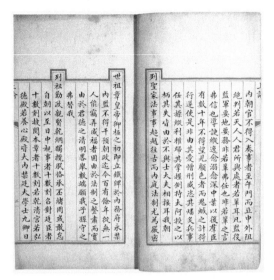

Manuscripts of the *History of the Qing Court*, red silk-lined version from 1736–1795.

The boundary was usually thicker outside and thinner inside.

Boundary line: Lines to mark outlines, lines painted with black, red and blue ink are called "black thread line," "red thread line" and "blue thread line," named thanks to the thin boundary line.

Head and foot: The upper part outside a typeface is the head. The bottom is the foot.

Heart: A narrow line in the centre of the typeface.

Fish tail: A graphic resembling a fish tail about a quarter of the way to the centre of the heart. The fish tail divides the heart into three parts. The centre is for the title, number of volume and page number. The upper part is for the page number and later book title - sometimes the publisher's name also appears here. The lower part for the type carver's name and, later, the publisher's name or name of the book series.

Trunk: The part between the fish tail and the frame. The trunk printed with black lines was called "heikou." It is called "xi heikou" if the line is thin and "cu heikou" if it is thick. In the absence of line or character, it is called "baikou."

Ear: Small box at the upper part of the boundary lines, usually for the name of the passage.

Structure of printed editions

Book clothes: Now called the cover, usually made using colored hard paper to protect the book, hence the name.

Book mark: Paper mark used to write the book title and pasted on the book clothes, usually inscribed by famous calligraphers or teachers.

Protection page: Also called title page, it is a blank page inside the book.

Cover page: Cover in ancient times referred to the first page after the protection page. The title was written on it, usually by someone famous.

Book spine: One end of the binding, also called book back.

Book mouth: The opposite side of the spine.

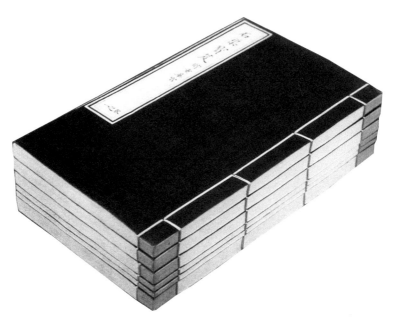

Wrapped corner of the stitched bound *Shiqu Baoji* manuscript from 1736–1795.

Book brain: Places where holes are punched for thread to go through. In modern hard-cover editions, the places where staples go are also called the book brain,

Book head: Refers to the cut on the top of the book.

Book root: Refers to the cut at the bottom.

Wrapped corner: Corners wrapped with silk, to protect the book and to make it look neat.

The Course of Inheritance
Collection, Preservation and Spread of Chinese Books

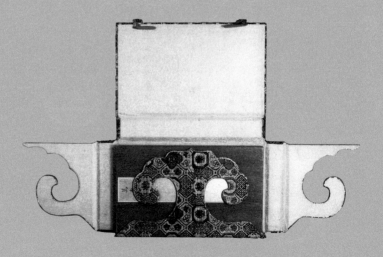

Over thousands of years of the publishing industry in China, the number and variety of books continued to grow alongside the development of society and culture. At the same time, man-made destruction (bans, war, theft) and natural disasters (water, fire, insects), and other factors led to the loss and disappearance of books. Such loss is very serious. A number of major book disasters caused immeasurable loss to ancient Chinese culture. To address this issue, the ancient Chinese invented various ways to preserve books. Their efforts gave rise to the colorful and time-honored history of collection. The history of book collecting in China, from management of oracle records during the Shang and Zhou dynasties to the emergence of modern libraries in the early twentieth century, is over 3,000 years old.

Jiayetang Library in Huzhou, Zhejiang, completed in 1924, which is strongly reminiscent of a traditional collection house.

In general, book-collecting in ancient China was intended for book preservation rather than circulation, which makes a certain distinction between book-collecting houses and libraries in modern times. The publishing industry in ancient China, mainly circulating through sale in book markets, transcription and borrowing, formed the book trade and shaped the famed "book road" of exchange between publishing industries at home and abroad.

Bibliophiles and Book-Collecting

Book collection in ancient China can be divided into four categories: Official collection, private collection, temple collection and college collection. As a main channel for the protection of ancient books and records, the first two achieved greater success. Traditional book collectors are private while "Changshulou," or book collection houses, are structures used for book preservation, including those run by official organizations, private groups or individuals. In ancient China, the mainstay of book collection, management, research and publication is official and non-official libraries. These buildings, together with the collectors linked to them, preserved and spread a wealth of ancient books and records and the history and culture of China.

Book collection in ancient China started during the Xia and Shang dynasties. Unearthed oracle bones from Anyang in Henan Province show that Shang period historiographers and shamans were already aware of the importance of preserving and colleting documents and literature. The collection of oracle bones was the earliest form of book collecting.

Formal book collection started in the Zhou Dynasty. The book-collecting institutions in the period bore names such as "Tianfu," "Mengfu," "Cefu," "Zhoufu," "Storehouse" and "Privy Chambers," with various positions, divided into "Mahavamsa," "Xiaoshi," "Neishi," "Waishi," "Zuoshi" and "Youshi," for the historiographers in charge, reflecting the scale and divisions of the official collection institutions in the Zhou Dynasty. It is reported that the famous thinker Laozi once worked as a historiographer of the Zhou Dynasty's "Cangshi," the

Image of Laozi, who was once an official in the Zhou Dynasty's state collection agency, and is known as the earliest curator of China's national library.

equivalent to a curator of a national library nowadays. There are several known private book collectors from the period, including the famous scholar Hui Shi (370–310B.C.) who had five carriages of books, a huge collection at the time.

Despite the first emperor's order to burn and destroy books after the unification of the country, official book collecting never stopped. During his reign, several book collection organizations were set up in the Erpang Palace in Xianyang, such as Mingtang and Shishi. Specific officials were designated to manage them. Resistance to the imperial order to destroy books was widespread as various ways were invented to preserve books. It was against this background that the story of keeping books in Eryou unfolds. According to the story, at the end of the

列朝人書畫目錄
書冊上等
宋四家集冊
宋元寶翰
元人法書

石渠寶笈卷之二

貯重華宮

天一 地一 元一

Shiqu Baoji, imperial court manuscript, the title indicates the continued influence of the Han Dynasty's collection houses.

Qin Dynasty, to avoid damage from war, a scholar moved all his books to caves in Dayou and Eryou Hills in Hunan Province. Generations later they were found. These books were called the "collection from the Eryou stone chambers." A Ming scholar, Hu Yinglin (1551–1602), touched by ancestral passion for books and study, named his book collection room "Eryou Shanfang."

In the early days of the Western Han period, the minister Xiao He (?–193 B.C.) presided over the construction of three imperial libraries, called Shiquge, Tianluge and Qilinge, to collect books and archives. Later, Shiqu and Tianlu became another name for imperial collections. As an attempt to protect books from fire and water, libraries in the Han Dynasty were made of stone and called "Shishi" or stone chambers. The bookcases were coated with copper sheet and called "Jinkui" or golden casket. Afterwards, these two names became terms for the structures used to house imperial books collections. A group of famous book collectors also emerged during the Han Dynasty.

After the founding of the Eastern Han Dynasty, book collection resumed and books were kept in Dongguan, Lantai and some other locations. At the peak of collection, there were enough

The Tianyige outlook, the earliest existing private collection house in China.

books to fill over 6,000 carts. Of the seven libraries in this period, the most famous ones are Lantai and Dongguan, which played a role in proofreading, editing and writing besides their part in collecting books. In 159A.D., the first organization in the feudal central government, in charge of book collection and proofreading, was set up. The "Archival Bureau," as it was called, functioned for 1,500 years.

Although books could not expect to be immune from constant turmoil and wars that took place during the Three Kingdoms, the Jin Dynasty and Northern and Southern Dynasties, rulers gradually realized the significance and value of collecting books. By then, the main collector was the "Archival Bureau." During the Sui Dynasty, two emperors once ordered fifty copies of each sort of book to be made from their extensive collection and the copies were sheltered in the Guanwendian in the capital of

Luoyang. Another location with a high concentration of books was Chang'an, where 370,000 rolls of books were deposited in Jiazedian.

By the Tang Dynasty, the management of books was quite developed and libraries also took up functions of editing and proofreading. Most books were collected in the Archival Bureau and managed by the director of the Archival Bureau. In addition, there were Hongwenguan, Shiguan, Jixianguan (collectively called Sanguan) as well as Chongwenyuan, Sijingyuan and Hanlinyuan, which were independent but closely related to each other. For example, the major function of Hongwenguan was to collect and proofread books; Shiguan was responsible for book writing and collection, set up in the Zhenguan period; Jixianyuan was the largest state library in the mid-Tang Dynasty and also the most complete with a collection exceeding any other. Chongwenyuan was a school set up for princes in the Zhenguan period, but also functioned in terms of book collection, proofreading and transcription; Sijingju, providing services for princes, was an organization in charge of book affairs in the East Palace; Hanlinyuan was a consulting organization used to

Huangshicheng and jinkui inside the deposited archives.

Outlook of the Iron Qin Bronze Sword Tower of the Quís in Changshu, Jiangsu.

draft emperors' ordinances, and book collection was meant to assist this function. This system of collecting had far-reaching influence on following generations. During this dynasty, the number of private collectors was larger than the sum of previous generations.

The spread of woodblock printing promoted the development of official and private book collections during the Song and Yuan dynasties. During the Song, the national collection agencies were Shiguan, Zhaowenguan, Jixianyuan and later Chongwenguan, which was built on the collection efforts from the three earlier agencies. In addition, there were other agencies like Mige, Taiqinglou and Liuge. Among them, Mige housed some 10,000 volumes selected from the three agencies, which represented the essence of the national library. College and private collections were well developed during the Song Dynasty, the well-known bibliophiles, Ye Mengde (1077–1148), Chao Gongwu (1105–1180), Zheng Qiao (1104–1162), Chen Zhensun (c.1183–1262) and

Outlook of Guyue Library in Shaoxing, Zhejiang, the first public library in the modern history of China.

others - each had collections with more than 10,000 volumes. In addition, the preparation of private collection catalogues witnessed a series of breakthroughs, which made private collections more academic. During the Yuan Dynasty, specialized agencies in charge of printing were placed under the supervision of the archival bureau. State collection during the Yuan Dynasty inherited features from the Southern Song, putting equal emphasis on both manuscripts and printed versions.

Academic and cultural prosperity during the Ming Dynasty, combined with more developments in printing, helped official and private collections prosper beyond those of previous generations. During the Ming Dynasty, the national collection agency was Wenyuange. The independent specialized state agency of book supervision was the archival bureau, later replaced by the Hanlinyuan. In addition, in 1534, the Ming Dynasty built an archive warehouse for imperial files and works called Huangshicheng. This was the most complete existing imperial library complex. During this period, private collection was very popular and the size of libraries also expanded. Most collectors were to be found in the economicly and culturally prosperous south-east. One of the most prestigious private libraries was the Tianyi Pavilion of the Fans in Ningbo, Jiguge of the Maos in Changshu and Danshengtang of the Qis in Shanyin. Built in 1561, during the Ming Dynasty, Tianyige housed 70,000 volumes and survives to this day. It is the earliest private library still in existence in China.

Most state collections during the Qing Dynasty were housed in the inner imperial court, in Huangshicheng, Zhaorendian, Wuyingdian, Chizaotang, Yangxindian, Nanxundian, Ziguangge and Nanshufang. The seven copies of *Siku Quanshu* compiled during Qianlong's reign were deposited in seven different places. The three in the south were open to students, which made them function like public libraries.

Of the 1,175 collectors recorded by scholar Ye Changchi (1849–1931) in his *Poems about Collecting Books*, 497 were from the Qing Dynasty. During the middle of the Qing Dynasty, four famous libraries emerged: Haiyuange by Yang Yizeng in Liaocheng, Iron Qin Bronze Sword Tower by Qu Shaoji in Changshu, Bisonglou by Lu Xinyuan in Gui'an and 8,000-Roll Tower by Ding Shen and Ding Bing in Hangzhou. The four libraries possessed many precious books from the Song and Yuan dynasties. Even after damage from wars and fire, Haiyuange still had over 219,000 volumes.

In the early twentieth century, with the introduction of modern libraries from the West, the traditional Chinese libraries gradually declined. Some opened their doors to the public, transforming themselves into modern libraries and ending the ancient Chinese tradition of private library undertakings.

Effective Ways to Protect Books

Over the long history of imperial and private book collection, special attention was given to the protection of books. Therefore, a complete set of techniques and methods were developed, which are still useful today. Generally, in order to address theft, tainting and other human damage, the following two approaches would be involved:

The first was classified arrangement and management. Some books were arranged according to content. For example, in Guanwendian, during the Sui Dynasty, Confucian classics and history books were kept in the east chamber; philosophy and literature books in the west chamber. The Tang-Dynasty book collector Li Bi used red toothpicks to mark Confucian classics, green for history, blue for philosophy and white for literature. Some arranged books according to quality. For example, book collection agencies in the Sui Dynasty used red glaze scrolls for

A corner of the rare book section in Shouan Palace of the Forbidden City.

Baoshulou, one scene in Tianyige.

the best quality books, black and red for ordinary books and black for sub-standard books. Similarly, in modern libraries, books are also classified as rare and ordinary editions. Some managed books based on their function. For example, Liu Gongchuo (763–830) from the Tang Dynasty had over 10,000 volumes and each one had three different versions, the best one deposited, a medium quality one for daily reading and lesser quality ones for beginners to use. Such classification shows unique insight to facilitate both the use and protection of books.

The second was strict restrictions on readers. Encouraged by the value of their possessions, private and official libraries were generally closed to the public, making them quite inaccessible. For example, the imperial collection was not supposed to be read by ordinary people; even senior officials had to follow very strict rules. Private collectors adopted a similar practice. For example, during the Ming Dynasty, Fan Qin (1506–1585) made it an explicit family rule that the books in Tianyige were not for lending and not to be taken outside the building. He had each and every one of his sons hold one key to the book house. Only when every son was present could the lock be opened. Books were not lent to outsiders; anyone within the family who wanted to read could do so inside the house during daytime. Smoking was strictly prohibited. Some other collectors allowed lending or outsiders in their library but with very stringent rules attached. For example, the book collector Ye Dehui (1864–1927) made it clear that no-one could go inside his library without him. No servants were allowed to follow. Winter coats or loose clothing were not allowed inside the library. Long conversations had to be held outside.

These rules may have their limitations but they served as some kind of protection for the books and avoided losses and theft.

Natural hazards to books are fire, water and insects. Against these problems ancient preservation techniques were also soundly developed. The main methods were as follows:

Architectural protection

Artistic values and practical functions were ingeniously integrated in the buildings of many ancient libraries. For example, "Shishi" and "Jinkui" in the Han Dynasty were designed as a measure against fire. In terms of architectural protection, the design and construct of Tianyige in the Ming Dynasty was also advanced for its time. Tianyige has two floors, the one above is a complete hall; the one below is separated into six chambers to prevent moisture damage. All the books are deposited on the upper floor with windows at the front and back. Shelves were well spaced and doors were placed in front and behind the book cabinets for ventilation. Insecticidal herbs were also placed in cabinets. To prevent fires, a pond was dug in front of the library, called Tianyi Pond.

In this way much damage caused by natural hazards was efficiently reduced.

Dyed paper

Even in the days of bamboo and wood strips, the treatment of drying green bamboo strips on the fire, "Shaqing,"was used to extend the life of bamboo strips. After the invention of paper, dying was used in order to protect the paper from insects and worms.

As early as the Han and Wei periods, people used juice from boiled *huangbo* or cork to stain paper and protect it from insects. This dyeing process is called *ruhuang* and it gives the paper a slightly yellow tint. For example, most of the sutras preserved in the Dunhuang Grottoes from the Tang Dynasty were stained yellow. Despite some broken parts, the paper is in good condition without any worm damage after over 1,000 years.

During the Song Dynasty, a new method was invented. Paper was soaked in a Sichuan pepper solution. The chemical composition and strong pungent odor of the pepper have a repellent effect on worms. During the Ming and Qing dynasties, in order to prevent the bookworms caused by humid weather in the south, a special paper called "10,000-year red paper" or *wannian hongzhi* was invented. This type of paper was prepared by painting paper with lead oxide. It was often used in sealed papers or as backing. The white and red combination looks smart and also prevents worm damage.

Chemical approaches

Pest-control agents or insecticides were purposely placed in book stacks to prevent books from damage by bookworms. "*Qimin Yaoshu*" mentioned that musk and papaya could be placed on bookshelves to prevent worms. Later herb-of-grace (rue) was put in libraries to prevent insects. This is very effective and it is

Slipcase with *ruyi* and cloud pattern in the refined manuscript *Eighty-Year Birthday Celebration* from the Qing Dynasty.

still practiced today in some libraries. The ancients also placed realgar and lime under bookcases, and tobacco and cinnamon inside them to prevent book worms.

Layout protection

A spill of rolled paper, as well as thread, was used in book binding so that the books were still undispersed even when threads broke. Sandalwood and nanmu were also used to make book sheaths. In order to implement insect prevention and save wear and tear, high quality silky cloth was employed to package books.

In addition, people would also air books on the sunny and dry days in early spring or mid-autumn, which could help rid the books of moisture and insects. The aired books, when completely cooled, were put back into cabinets afterwards. There were many factors to consider with regards to timing and ways of airing.

The Circulation of Ancient Books

The rise of civil bookstores marked the formal start of the book trade in ancient China. After the spread of printing techniques, the book trade shaped a huge book-distributing network system and created numerous trade centers.

Extravagant gold plated bookcase for "homage to the Bodhisattva Manjusri".

Bookstore and "Huaishi"

Not later than the later period of the 1st century B.C, the earliest civil bookstore in Chinese history emerged in the capital Chang'an, with others appearing in some economically and culturally developed cities.

The bookstores were run by civil merchants for profit, and a variety of books, open-selling and free-reading, not only attracted

Pushuting or "book-airing pavilion" owned by Zhu Yizun, a private collector from the Qing Dynasty in Jiaxing, Zhejiang.

readers but also met the study needs of poor intellectuals. These stores played the part of a public library, which did not exist at the time, and were well received by readers. Historical documents have many stories about famous scholars using book stores in this way. It is said that the famous scholar Wang Chong (27–c.97 A.D.) could not afford books because of his poor family background and was a frequent reader in bookstore.

The emergence of numerous bookstores, facilitating book circulation and utility, was also an important means to supplement official and individual book collections. In the process, the business of bookstores boomed, with the operation of mobile and home book services, and manifested an enriched flavor of commerciality. Stimulated by commercial profit, book peddlers at the time carried books to the gathering places of Confucian scholars, which gradually led to the creation of book markets.

From the end of the Western Han Dynasty (1–8 A.D.) to the Xin Dynasty (9–23 A.D.), the earliest book market, "Huaishi," in ancient China could be found near the Imperial College in Chang'an city. At the end of the Western Han Dynasty, when Wang Mang was in power, the Imperial College was enlarged, increasing the number of college students and assigning numerous scholars to hold official posts in the capital. The gathering of scholars and students promoted the demand of books and a comprehensive market including book trade was formed near the Imperial College. The market was called "Huaishi" after the several hundreds of locust trees found there.

Different from a civil bookstore, the "Huaishi" bore the following distinctive features. The first was its regularity. The market was held twice a month. Second, the main consumers were college students in Chang'an. Third, the buying and selling of goods also included musical instruments, locally grown products and suchlike. Fourth, communication and the exchange of learning characterized the market and academic discussions were frequently held there. Finally, "Huaishi" was under official supervision - a specialized institution set by the government monitored the "Huaishi." In 23 A.D., Wang Mang's regime collapsed. With the Imperial College dissolved, the "Huaishi" vanished. Although it survived for only twenty years, the "Huaishi" still exerted a great far-reaching influence on history. The "Huaishi" was often remembered as a cultural icon in poems by poets and scholars of later generations.

Book duplicator: "Yongshu"

Before the invention of engraving printing techniques, all books were manually copied; the process was both a continuation of book production and a manifestation of book circulation. In the Han dynasty there were persons employed as transcribers, known as *Yongshu*. The government at the time employed a great many *Yongshu* to copy books.

Being paid a comfortable salary, *Yongshu* at the time could at least manage to support a family. During the copying process, the *Yongshu* accumulated a lot of knowledge for fame. The famous general Ban Chao (32–102 A.D.), one of numerous *Yongshu* in the Eastern Han Dynasty, was poor when he was young. He was frequently employed by government organizations to earn money to support his aged mother. Once, when copying books, he suddenly cast away his writing brush, sighing, because a great man should fight on the battlefield to build his fame - how could he do this through long-term book copying? With great effort, Ban Chao went on to become a famous general. This led to the idea of "giving up civilian pursuits to join the army" in Chinese history.

"Proofreading Scene," drawn in the Northern Qi Dynasty (550–577) (this is a copy from the Song Dynasty), mirroring the state of book copying and proofreading at the time.

Book copying by numerous *Yongshu*, promoting book reproduction at the time, contributed significantly to the spread of cultural knowledge. It was a publishing phenomenon of manual duplicating work.

Bookstores with printing works

During the printing age, book distribution and circulation in China enjoyed tremendous growth. Thanks to the spread of printing techniques, printed books swarmed into society and became the best-selling books. Drawn by the profits to be made, more civilians and officials became devoted to book production and trade.

In the printing age, bookstores with printing works run by the civil booksellers played a major part in the book trade. Fulfilling a number of roles, these stores included an engraving, printing and selling business. Their primary mission and purpose were rapidly selling books in large quantities. With the emergence

Modern Liulichang in Beijing, once a famed national book trading market in Qing Dynasty and the Republic of China.

of more bookstores with printing works came competition. Therefore, business promotion was high on the owners' agendas. Numerous versions of the same book appeared in the same market at nearly the same time and there was a great increase in advertisements. In addition, some booksellers travelled to sell books, some doing trade in minority areas or abroad.

At that time, not only civil professional booksellers but also many scholars, government officials and average people were involved in the book trade in succession. The Confucian philosopher, Zhu Xi in the Song Dynasty (1130–1200) once printed Confucian classics and wrote books for selling and sold them from door to door.

The prosperity of the book trade helped to shape the national book market. Xiangguo Temple in Kaifeng city in the Northern Song Dynasty, Three Hills Street in Nanjing city in the Ming Dynasty and Liulichang in Beijing city in the Qing Dynasty became tremendous, prosperous book markets, and famed national trading centers in China.

Crystallization of Chinese Culture
Distinctive Chinese Publications

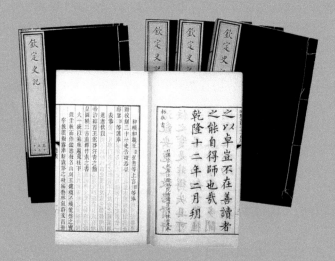

Ancient Chinese books, the most significant and direct output of ancient Chinese publishing, are good indicators of the tremendous number of publications that were handwritten or printed before 1911. By a conservative estimate there were no less than 100,000 different ancient books. Ancient Chinese books, embodying a concentrated reflection of the splendor of Chinese history and culture, are not only a flourishing symbol of the Chinese publishing industry, but also a crystallization of ancient Chinese wisdom and traditional culture.

From the seventh century onwards, ancient Chinese books were classified into four categories: *Jing, Shi, Zi* and *Ji*. "The Thirteen Confucian Classics" are part of *"Jing,"* the "Twenty-five Histories" are *"Shi,"* the "Selected Readings of Confucian and other Ancient Chinese Classics" are *"Zi"* and the "Poems and Prose Works" are *"Ji,"* together they offer a concentrated reflection of the characteristics of Chinese culture. In addition, numerous large reference books and series books bore another feature of broad Chinese culture. Among them, the *Yongle Encyclopedia* and *The Compendium of Works of the Past and the Present* are reference books and the *Siku Quanshu* are series books, both typical representatives of the brilliant achievements of China's ancient publishing industry.

The publishing industry in contemporary China continues the fine traditions of the ancient publishing industry. It publishes and republishes more than 100,000 different books every year. Among them are numerous outstanding publications that represent the level of publishing and cultural achievement of today's China such as *Revised Continuation of Siku Quanshu, Zhonghua Dazang Jing* (an encyclopedia of Tibetan studies in 150 volumes), *Encyclopedia of China.*

The Thirteen Confucian Classics

In the 2,000-plus years of feudal society, Confucian culture occupied a leading place in China. Confucian works were believed to be decidedly superior to others, so works about the study and interpretation of Confucian classics came out in massive numbers, shaping the unique study of "Confucian Classics."

"Confucian Classics" are books compiled by Confucians with Confucius as their representative and were generally endorsed by feudal Chinese governments. The academic system was formed by the remarks and themes of feudal governments, intellectuals and bureaucrats throughout the dynasties. As a result, there is a peculiar phenomenon in Chinese cultural history and Chinese book history, which is the belief that the "study of Confucian classics is superior, other learning is inferior; the study of Confucian classics is the main theme and other studies are sub-themes."

The rubbing of "Confucius Teaching." Confucius was the founder of Confucianism and is closely associated with Confucian Classics.

In ancient China, there were thirteen works known as the *Thirteen Confucian Classics*, regarded as the most important texts for the study of Confucianism. They were *I Ching*, *Shangshu*, *The Book of Odes*, *The Chou Rituals*, *Book Ceremony and Ritual*, *The Book of Rites*, *Zuo's Commentary of the Spring and Autumn Annals*, *The Gongyang Commentary of the Spring and Autumn Annals*, *The Guliang Commentary of the Spring and Autumn Annals*, *The Analects of Confucius*, *The Book of Filial Piety*, *Erya* and *Mencius*.

With these works as the focus, a large number of derivative works about the study of Confucian classics emerged. The *Thirteen Confucian Classics* total 650,000 words. There

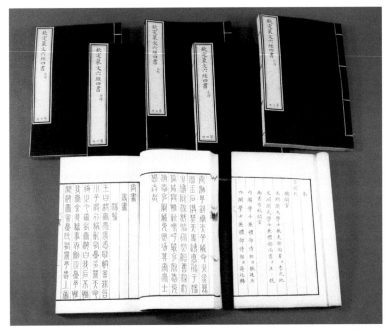

A carved copy of the *Seal Characters of the Six Confucian Classics and the Four Books*, from the reign of Emperor Kangxi of the Qing Dynasty.
The *Four Books* refers to the books comprising *The Great Learning*, *The Doctrine of the Mean*, *The Analects of Confucius* and *Mencius*.

are more than 4,000 books with 50,000 volumes dedicated to interpreting these classics. These interpretations represent some of the most important ancient Chinese books.

The *Thirteen Confucian Classics*, as the core works of Confucian culture, are among the most significant works of the traditional Chinese academy. The *I Ching*, the highest in rank, is given priority over the others. Originally a book of divination, it is based on the "Yin, Yang and Eight Diagrams," concepts which are profoundly imbedded in Chinese philosophy.

The *Shangshu* documents ancient times. Its main component is royal proclamations and minutes of talks between the emperor and his subjects. It also shows the impact of the "Five Elements"

(gold, wood, water, fire and earth) on Chinese thinking.

The Book of Odes, dating from the early Western Zhou Dynasty to the middle of the Spring and Autumn Period, contains the earliest poetic syllogism in China. It is regarded as the model for tradition Chinese poems, which include *The Ballads*, *The Dynastic Hymns*, and *The Sacrificial Songs*. *The Ballads* refers to the chants of the vassal states during the Zhou Dynasty; the Dynastic Hymns includes court music and part of the rites and music in the territory controlled Zhou Dynasty; the Sacrificial Songs described sacred dance music and poems for the upper classes in the ancestral temple.

The majestic carved copy of the *Annotation of the Classics of the Spring and Autumn Period* in the Shu Area (now Sichuan Province) during the Song Dynasty.

The Chou Rituals, *The Book of Ceremony and Ritual* and *The Book of Rites*, which settle moral principles in traditional Chinese society, are called the "Three Etiquettes." *The Chou Rituals* records the practices of bureaucratic establishments in the Zhou Dynasty and various states' systems in the Warring States Period; *The Book Ceremony and Ritual* records the etiquette system of the Spring and Autumn and the Warring States Periods; *The Book of Rites* compiles works about various etiquettes before the Qin and Han dynasties.

Zuo's Commentary of the Spring and Autumn Annals, *The Gongyang Commentary of the Spring and Autumn Annals* and *The Guliang Commentary of the Spring and Autumn Annals*, which are formed around "The Spring and Autumn Annals," are called the "Three Records of the Spring and Autumn Annals." *The Spring*

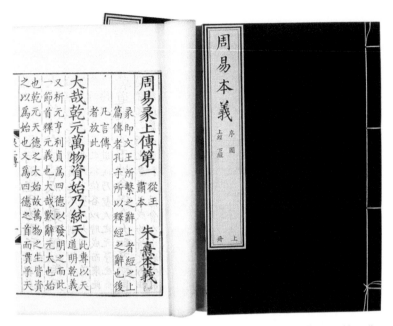

The imperial-court carved copy of *The Original Meaning of I Ching* during Emperor Kangxi's reign during the Qing Dynasty.

and Autumn Annals is an annalistic history based on the book of the Lu State by Confucius.

Zuo's Commentary of the Spring and Autumn Annals focuses on historical events in *The Spring and Autumn Annals*. It also aims to elucidate the arguments in *The Spring and Autumn Annals*. *The Analects of Confucius*, the most widely read Confucian classic in ancient China, records the words and deeds of Confucius and his disciples - it is the most magisterial account of Confucianism.

The Book of Filial Piety is based on the idea of governing with filial piety. It discusses feudal filial duty. It is the only Confucian classic in *The Thirteen Classics, Annotated and Explicated* annotated by Emperor Xuanzong of the Tang Dynasty. *Erya,* an book of interpretation that explains word meanings and annotates names and descriptions, is the only ancient lexicon regarded as a classic in ancient China by scholars of Confucian classics.

Mencius is devoted to the great thinker Mencius' words, thought and deeds, whose central idea was the promotion of a policy of benevolence.

The History of the Twenty-Five Dynasties

Worship of the past and an emphasis on history is a notable feature of Chinese culture. Generations of rulers in China attached great importance to the continuity and succession of ancient history and maintained a tradition of recording the history of the previous dynasty. The system ensured the consistency and continuity of history books. Privately written history books were also very popular. History books rank below books in the *Jing* category but far exceed them in terms of total number, type, variety and style.

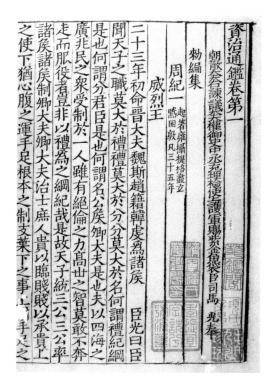

The Gongshiku edition of the *Comprehensive Mirror for the Aid of Government*, the masterpiece of Chinese chronicles from the Song Dynasty during the reign of Emperor Gaozong.

History books from ancient China come mainly in three types: Character-centered biographies, chronological records of history and event-centered chronicles. Among them, *The Records of the Grand Historian* is regarded as an official edition. Emperor Qianlong designated it and histories of twenty-three

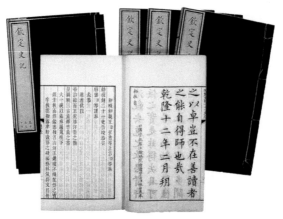

The Records of the Grand Historian, one of twenty-four historical books printed during the reign of Emperor Qianlong of the Qing Dynasty.

dynasties, including the *History of the Ming Dynasty* completed in 1739, as the *Histories of the Twenty-Four Dynasties*, making them official. The completion of the *Draft History of the Qing Dynasty* in 1927 added a twenty-fifth to this collection. Together, they include 3,795 volumes, recording history from the legendary Yellow Emperor to 1911, making an unparalleled encyclopedia of Chinese history.

The *History of Twenty-Five Dynasties* is presented as a series of biographies that chronicle historical events. In terms of style, the biographies can be divided into "Benji," "Shijia," "Liezhuan," "Shuzhi" and "Shibiao."

Benji refers to the chronological record of imperial deeds; *Shijia* to histories of noted families; *Liezhuan* to biographies; *Shuzhi* to other histories of diverse institutions, systems, nature and society; and *Shibiao* to historical lists of intricate social circumstances and figures that are not included in other biographies. These five sections interact and combine to form the whole history.

The Earliest Biographical Work of Ancient History in China: The Records of the Grand Historian

The Records of the Grand Historian, the earliest biographical work of ancient history in China, written by Sima Qian (145–90B.C.), a famous Western Han historian, is also considered the finest historical book in China. Leading the "Twenty-Four Histories," The Records of the Grand Historian, also called Tai Shi Gong Shu, covers a history of 3,000 years from the legendary Huang Di, or Yellow Emperor, to the first year of Yuanshou Period of Emperor Wudi of the Han Dynasty (122 B.C.), it consists of 130 volumes with 520 thousand words. The biographical historiography that originated with the book was followed by later official histories and a far-reaching influence on the later development of history and literature, The Records of the Grand Historian also occupies an important position in Chinese literary history.

Yongle Encyclopedia

Leishu, or reference books, are also special. These books collect all the materials related to a certain category and compile them by category to facilitate searching and citing. Because of their wide coverage and rich information these were known as the encyclopedias of ancient times. The first reference book, *The Imperial Reader*, was compiled in 220 A.D. It included more than forty categories with over eight million words. By the end of the nineteenth century, over 700 reference books had been put together. The largest was the *Yongle Encyclopedia* and the most complete was *The Compendium of Works of the Past and the Present*.

The *Yongle Encyclopedia* was commissioned in 1403 (the sixth year of the reign of Emperor Chengzu of the Ming Dynasty, whose imperial title was Yongle) and completed five years later. All together, 2,169 people were involved in the compilation. More than 1,300 were involved just in the transcription. It is one of the best-known manuscripts from the peak of block printing. It includes 22,937 manuscript rolls, 11,095 volumes and about 370 million Chinese characters, making it a true encyclopedia. Besides the impressive scale, all the characters were written in neat brush standard script decorated with many delicate illustrations, and punctuated in red. The pages were large, with a graceful yellow hardcover and in wrapped-back binding.

Unlike previous reference books, the *Yongle Encyclopedia* used rhyme to organize the first words, which facilitated retrieval. Based on the rhyme groups set out in *The Rhyme Dictionary of Hongwu*, the official rhymes dictionary compiled in the beginning of the Ming Dynasty, all characters in different rhyme groups were arranged in the *Yongle Encyclopedia*. Detailed explanations about the meanings of each character were given, followed by

Binding of the *Yongle Encyclopedia*.

A partial copy of extant *Yongle Encyclopedia*.

The entry for "门" in the *Yongle Encyclopedia*.

different ways of writing characters and summaries, allusions, poems, essays and so on. All the information about the characters was collected and listed and all quotations were from the original classics.

Quotations were written with a writing brush dipped in red ink, and other information was written with black ink. With a clear column structure, compiled in a way similar to the method used to this day, the *Yongle Encyclopedia* is regarded as the world's first and biggest encyclopedia.

The scope of the *Yongle Encyclopedia* is simply enormous. Over 7,000 ancient books were included, which pretty much covered the entire collection of the imperial book agency, Wenyuange, during the Ming Dynasty. The collection there included an array of subjects such as agriculture, art, astronomy, drama, geology, history, literature, medicine, natural sciences, religion and technology. The result was the creation of a "library" in the early years of the fifteenth century. Over 500 very rare books have been found in this encyclopedia by later generations. After it was completed, the *Yongle Encyclopedia* was kept in the imperial court and not circulated in print. It was eventually destroyed by fire and theft.

It is estimated that the surviving volumes of the *Yongle Encyclopedia* in libraries and private collections in China total just over 800 rolls and 400-plus volumes; less than 4% of the original.

The Compendium of Works of the Past and the Present

The largest and most complete officially compiled reference book in existence is *The Compendium of Works of the Past and the Present* published during the Qing Dynasty. This book has

10,040 rolls, 5,020 volumes in 525 sheaths and about 170 million characters. It also includes over 10,000 illustrations and 6,000 cited works.

Chen Menglei (1650–1741) and Jiang Tingxi (1669–1732) presided over the editing during the reigns of Kangxi and Yongzheng. Chen Menglei contributed most to this huge project. The editing took twenty-eight years and was completed in 1726. Emperor Yongzheng ordered sixty-five copies made from copper block type. They were completed in 1728 and were used as gifts for high government officials. The work was not circulated until 1890, when the Shanghai Tongwen Bookstore was commissioned by the inner court to make 100 copies in the original size. These copies were used as gifts to foreign countries.

Adhering to the rules of arrangement for reference books, summarized as "dividing things based on their categories," the overall structure of *The Compendium of Works of the Past and the Present* is based on a classification system designed on the basis of the traditional approach of "sky, earth, human, matter and thing," which is formed by *"Huibian," "Dian"* and *"Bu."* With a clear and meticulous system, it goes far beyond previous reference books and further develops the concept of "dividing things based on their categories." It represents a maturity in

Portrait of Qing Dynasty Emperor Kangxi reading.

Binding of *The Compendium of Works of the Past and the Present.*
The interior court copperplate edition of *Illustrations of the Compendium of Works of the Past and the Present* from the reign of Emperor Yongzheng of the Qing Dynasty.

the development of Chinese reference books. It is hailed as the "Kangxi Encyclopedia" or "Chinese Encyclopedia" and has long enjoyed great fame both at home and abroad.

Siku Quanshu and the Revised Continuation of Siku Quanshu

The compilation of book series started very early. Of all the book series, the one with the largest scale and biggest influence was the *Siku Quanshu*, officially compiled during the Qing Dynasty. The four branches refer to *Jing* classics, *Shi* histories, *Zi* philosophy works and *Ji* anthologies. The collection is complete, intact and diversified.

This enterprise started in 1772 and concluded in 1782. It covers 3,470 ancient books, 79,018 rolls in 36,078 volumes with approximately one-billion Chinese characters. It is about 44 times larger than the *Encyclopedia* edited by Diderot. To this day no book can challenge its scale.

Siku Quanshu covered all the most important cultural works of literature written before Emperor Qianlong's reign. In terms of coverage and magnitude, it was unprecedented not only in China but also in the world. Under the four categories there were sub-categories, including 10 under *Jing*, 15 under *shi*, 14 under *zi*, and 5 under *ji*. In all, there were 44 categories.

During the editing of *Siku Quanshu*, based on content, biographical notes, the origin of the literature and other information, the editors produced *The Outline of the Title Catalogue of Siku Quanshu* in 200 volumes, a great

Portrait of Emperor Qianlong in court dress.

collection of ancient catalogues. Its numerous volumes made it difficult to read, so Emperor Qianlong ordered officials to write a concise version of this title catalogue under the name *The Concise Title Catalogue of Siku Quangshu,* which included 20 volumes.

To store *Siku Quanshu*, Emperor Qianlong had seven buildings constructed, modeled after the famous Tianyige in Ningbo. They are collectively called seven chambers in the north and the south. The north libraries are Wenyuange in the Forbidden City, Wenyuange in the Old Summer Palace, Wensuge in Shenyang, and Wenjin Chamber in the Summer Resort of Chengde. These four imperial libraries were not open to the public.

The three south libraries are Wenlange in Hangzhou, Wenhuige in Yangzhou and Wenzongge in Zhenjiang, which were open to intellectuals for reading and transcribing. Currently four of the seven copies of *Siku Quanshu* are preserved in the China National Library (Wenjinge), Taiwan Library

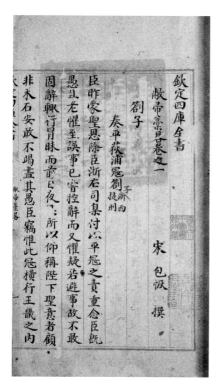

臣昨蒙聖恩除臣浙右司集付以平寇之責重念臣既

欽定四庫全書

敬帝豪見甲卷之一

劉子

奏平蒞浦冦劉子^{浙西提刑}

宋 包恢 撰

Handwritten edition of *Literary Essays of the Siku Quanshu* by the Imperial Academy.

(Wenyuange), Gansu Provincial Library (Wensuge) and Zhejiang Provincial Library (Wenlange). Three other copies were destroyed in war in the 1860s.

The copied books in *Siku Quanshu* have neat calligraphy, clear painting and wonderful binding. Books belonging to *Jing, Shi, Zi* and *Ji*—or classical, historical, philosophical and *belles-lettres* are covered by silks of different colors. Green, red, blue and grey represent four categories. Classics were covered in green silk, historical works in red, works of philosophy in blue and *belles-lettres* in grey. Several volumes of books are stored in a delicate case made of *nanmu*. The frame of each volume is red with the four characters for *Siku Quanshu* in the middle of the cover. Below the title *Siku Quanshu* was the name of the copied book, the serial number of the volume and the page number. Each volume has its own summary at the beginning.

It should be noted that in the process of compiling *Siku Quanshu*, many books that were regarded as harmful to Emperor Qianlong's rule were either deleted or destroyed, which distorted many precious works and simply made them disappear. Still *Siku Quanshu* had some positive impact. On the whole, the completion of *Siku Quanshu* highlighted the ambition of the Chinese nation and the wisdom - as well as the stigmatization - of scholars. Arguably, the Great Wall, the Grand Canal, and *Siku Quanshu* represent the most precious parts of China's heritage.

Wenlange Tower in Hangzhou Zhejiang, the only surviving part of the Nan San Ge.

China launched the continuation of *Siku Quanshu* in 1994. All 1,800 volumes were written and edited over eight years. It was published in 2002 by Shanghai Classics Publishing House. The collection of *Revised Continuation of Siku Quanshu* includes classics published before and after *Siku Quanshu* went into circulation; that is 5,213 classics, an increase of 51% compared with the original *Siku Quanshu*.

The best edition of each book was chosen as the basis. Following the style of *Siku Quanshu*, the *Revised Continuation of Siku Quanshu* is divided according to *Jing, Shi, Zi* and *Ji* and categories are marked with the colors green, red, blue and grey. There are 1,800 hardback copies of books printed in A4 format, 260 of which are *Jing* or classical works, 670 *Shi* or historical works, 370 *Zi* or philosophical works and 500 *Ji* or belles-lettres. This book and the original *Siku Quanshu* form a large collection of significant Chinese classics published before 1911.

Manuscript edition of the *Concise Bibliography of the Siku Quanshu* and its case.

Poetry Anthologies of the Tang Dynasty: *Complete Collection of Tang Poetry* and *Three Hundred Tang Poems*

China is known as the homeland of poetry. Poetry has always been an important form of traditional Chinese literature. Ancient Chinese poetry, or classical Chinese poetry, refers to poetry created in classical Chinese based on certain rules and forms. In a broad sense, ancient poetry includes many ancient Chinese verses such as *Fu, Ci* and *Qu* and so on; while in a narrow sense, it includes ancient-style poetry and "modern style" poetry. Tang Poetry, Song *Ci* and Yuan *Qu* respectively represent the greatest accomplishment in Chinese poetic history.

The Tang Dynasty (618–907) was the most splendid and prosperous time for Chinese ancient poetry. Tang Poetry stands as the pinnacle of ancient Chinese poetry. Based on conclusions by the scholar Cheng Yuzhui, the prosperity of Tang Poetry can be demonstrated in six ways. First, the quantity of poems

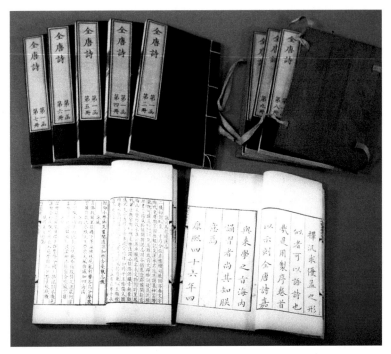

The Complete Collection of Tang Poetry published by the Poetry Institution of Yangzhou during the reign of Emperor Kangxi of the Qing Dynasty.

produced, at more than 50,000, is unparalleled. Second, Tang poetry included an unprecedented number of poets from a wide range of social classes, many of whom are famous. Third, Tang poetry was created from various schools of poetry and focused on a wide range of subjects and styles. Fourth, Tang Poetry consists of different types of poems such as *Yue Fu* or folk poetry, *Wu Jue* or classical poems with four five-character lines, *Qi Jue* or septasyllabic poetry, *Wu Lü* or classical poems with eight five-character lines, *Qi Lü* or septasyllabic regulated verse, and so forth. Fifth, Tang poetry includes numerous famous poems. Sixth, Tang Poetry reflects the creative spirit and pursuit of novelty and change that was a characteristic of the period.

Famous poets from the Tang Dynasty such as Li Bai, Du Fu, Bai Juyi, Wang Wei and Cen Shen all have extant collections of poems that have been widely read and recited by later generations. Most Tang poetry has been collected in the *Complete Collection of Tang Poetry* edited during the Qing Dynasty. This collection is considered a complete collection of Tang Poetry. Since the Tang Dynasty, selected works of Tang poetry have surfaced one after another, the most popular of which is the *Three Hundred Tang Poems,* edited by the Heng Tang Hermit or Sun Zhu.

The *Complete Collection of Tang Poetry,* the largest collection of the genre, is a complete collection of Tang Poetry works. It was edited in the early years of the Qing Dynasty by Cao Yin, Peng Dingqiu and others on orders from Emperor Kangxi. It contains 900 volumes. According to statistics by the Japanese scholar Hiraoka Takeo, there are 49,403 poems and 1,553 *Ju* by 2,873 writers in the *Complete Collection of Tang Poetry.* Editing started in May 1705 and finished in October 1706. The reason why it took such a short time to compile the collection was that scholars from past dynasties made great efforts to keep track of Tang poetry. Cao Yin and other scholars made full use of the achievements of their ancestors. Among these achievements, *Tang Yin Tong Qian* by Hu Zhenheng (1569–1645) from the Ming Dynasty and *Tang Poetry* by Ji Zhenyi (1630–1674) from the beginning of the Qing Dynasty were the most important.

The *Complete Collection of Tang Poetry* was printed and published by the inner court in the years after it was finished. The Poetry Institution of Yangzhou then published it. The two editions both contain 120 volumes and are split into 10 cases. Collecting Tang poetries into one book, the *Complete Collection of Tang Poetry* facilitates study, although there are some flaws in it due to the speed with which it was collected.

After the publication of this book, many supplements and textual criticisms were published in the later dynasties. Among them, the *Supplement of the Complete Collection of Tang Poetry* published by the Zhonghua Book Company was the most significant. Meanwhile, a complete electronic and a complete

The wooden-type print version of *Tangshi Leiyuan* from the reign of Emperor Shenzong of the Ming Dynasty, whose imperial title was Wanli.

network retrieval system for the *Complete Collection of Tang Poetry* has been established for readers' convenience.

Three Hundred Tang Poems by Heng Tang Hermit or Sun Zhu is the most popular selected work of Tang poems. Heng Tang Hermit's original name was Sun Zhu. He was from Wuxi, Jiangsu Province. He was a diligent, studious and incorruptible official. Because he thought there was a shortage of Tang poetry for beginners, he decided to edit a new collection suitable for private schools that could be handed down to later generations. He chose often-quoted and easy-to-read poems.

In 1765, the book was finished. There were 310 poems by 77 poets from the Tang Dynasty, 33 of which were *Wu Yan* or poems with five characters in each line, 46 were *Yue Fu* or folk poetry, 28 were *Qi Yan* or poems with seven characters in each line, 50 were *Qi Lü* or eight-line poems with seven characters per line and following rigorous prosodic rules, 29 were *Wu Jue* or classical poems with four five-character lines, 51 of which were *Qi Jue* or septasyllabic. Each of the poems was matched with an explanation and comment.

Opinions about the origin of the book title vary. Some say the title stemmed from a saying which read: "If you are familiar with three hundred Tang poems, you can recite poems even if you cannot compile them." Others say the title originated from *The Book of Odes*. After the book was published, it became so popular that almost every family has a copy and it has remained in print. For hundreds of years, it has maintained its popularity.

Ci Anthologies from the Song Dynasty: *Complete Collection of Song Ci*

Song *Ci*, a literary genre that appeared after the Tang, and Tang Poetry are known as the Two Excellencies of Literature. Both represent the pinnacle of literature from a particular dynasty. In terms of style, Song *Ci* can be divided into two schools as follows: One is graceful and restrained with Li Qingzhao, Liu Yong and Qin Guan and others as representatives; the other is bold and unconstrained with Xin Qiji, Su Shi and Chen Liang and others as representatives. The *Complete Collection of Song Ci* is the largest collection of Song Ci edited by contemporary Tang Guizhang.

The publication of *The Collection of Sixty Famous Ci Writers in The Song Dynasty* by the famous publisher Mao Jin at the end of the Ming Dynasty marked the beginning of the printing of

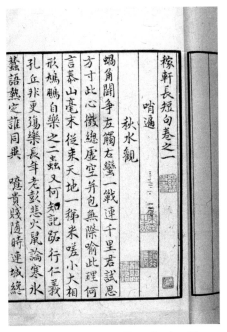

The carved copy of *Jiaxuan Changduanju or The Collection of Ci* by Xin Qiji published by Guangxin Book House in 1299.

Portrait of Tang Guizhang.

collections of *ci* writers of the Song Dynasty. After this, different collections by other editors in later dynasties were published. However, none of them could give a complete picture of the Song *Ci*.

In the 1930s, on the basis of different collections by different editors, Tang Guizhang collected and started to compile the *Complete Collection of Song Ci*. After seven years of hard work, his collection was finished and the Commercial Press published a thread-bound edition in 1940. After the founding of the PRC, Tang Guizhang started the supplement and revision of his book and the Zhonghua Book Company published a new edition in 1965.

There are more than 1,400 *ci* included as supplements in the new edition whose style is different from that of the old one. In the old edition, *ci* are arranged according to the classification of "Emperor" and "imperial clan"; while in the new one, it is arranged based on time with an index of authors at the end of the book. There are 20,000 *ci* by 1,330 writers from the Southern Song Dynasty and Northern Song Dynasty with more than 530 reference books.

After the publication of this new edition, the editor kept revising and supplementing the book and *The Supplement and Revision* was added to the end of the reprinted version of this book in 1979. In all, this book is an essential reference work for Song *Ci* research. Tang Guizhang set an outstanding example in the history of Chinese publishing.

Collections of Yuan *Qu*: *The Complete Collection of Yuan Sanqu* and *The Anthology of Yuan Qu*

With unique style in terms of thought, content and artistic achievement, Yuan *Qu* is an exquisite part of Chinese literature. It is on a par with Tang Poetry and Song *Ci*. As the main literature from the Yuan Dynasty, Yuan *Qu*, which contains *Zaju* and *Sanqu*, was not only literature for the educated and officials to express their feeling and ambitions but also a brand new artistic style popular among ordinary people. There are numerous writers of Yuan *Qu*, among whom are Guan Hanqing, Tang Xianzhu and Ji Junxiang. Their masterpieces are *Dou E's Grievance, West Chamber* and *The Little Orphan of the House of Chao*, which enjoy a high reputation in literary circles around the world.

The most famous collection is *The Anthology of Yuan Qu* edited by Zang Maoxun (1550–1620) during the Ming Dynasty. It collects 100 different kinds of Yuan Dramas in 100 volumes. The book is also known as *One Hundred Qu of Yuan People*. The number of extant Yuan Drama by Yuan people numbers less than 200 and more than half of them are collected in *The Anthology of Yuan Qu*, which focuses on well-known plays, such as *Dou E's Grievance* by Guan Hanqing, *Emperor Minghuang of Tang Dynasty and the Phoenix Tree on a Rainy Night in Autumn* by Bai Pu and *The Autumn in Han Palace* by Ma Zhiyuan and so on by different play writers.

Therefore, this book played a significant role in the spread of Yuan Drama. Sui Shusen, a contemporary scholar, collected Yuan *Zaju* found during the past decades and compiled *"The Supplement of the Anthology of Yuan Qu,"* which was published by Zhonghua Book Company in September 1959. In the above two books, *The Anthology of Yuan Qu* and *The Supplement of The Anthology of Yuan Qu*, all extant Yuan Dramas are collected.

The Anthology of Yuan Qu, edited by Sui Shushen in the contemporary era, is the most famous complete collection of Yuan Sanqu. It includes works from 213 authors, from Yuan Haowen of the Jin Dynasty to Gu Zijing at the end of the Yuan Dynasty and several anonymous works. There are over 3,800 *Xiaoling*, 450 *Taoqu* arranged in the authors' chronological sequence. With a short biography for each author and the source of each work, it provides a complete picture of the *Sanqu* in the Yuan Dynasty. Among the six volumes of *White Snow in Early Spring* collected by Luo Zhenyu and found recently by the library of Liaoning Province, there are twenty-five unseen *Tao Qu*, which can be seen as the supplement to *The Anthology of Yuan Qu*.

Novels in the Ming and Qing Dynasties: *Four Great Classical Novels* and *Three Collections and Short Stories*

The Ming and Qing dynasties were periods of prosperity for Chinese classical fiction. Novels from the Ming and Qing dynasties have unprecedented scope and depth. They mirror various aspects of social life at the time and became an important literary genre for people to understand their social environment and to entertain themselves. In Chinese literary history, they are considered parallel to Tang Poetry, Song *Ci* and Yuan *Qu*. Among them, the famous "Four Great Classical Novels," namely *Romance of the Three Kingdoms*, *Journey to the West*, *Water Margin* (also known as *Outlaws of the Marsh*) and *A Dream of Red Mansions*, are seen as precious cultural heritage.

Romance of the Three Kingdoms has 120 chapters and is based on *The History of the Three Kingdoms* by Chen Shou combined with folk tales. Luo Guanzhong completed it at the end of the Yuan Dynasty and the early Ming Dynasty (1330–1400). As the first Zhanghui-style novel in China, it has plain text, numerous impressive figures, an intricate plot and a vast narrative structure. It vividly describes the complicated military and political struggles among the Wei, Shu and Wu kingdoms during the end of the Eastern Han Dynasty and the Three Kingdoms Period.

Water Margin, by Shi Naian (1296–1371) or by Shi Naian and Luo Guanzhong, based on *Xuanhe Yishi* (a story book), depicts a majestic story of 108 people led by Song Jiang who are driven to revolt during the North Song Dynasty. As the first oral-language novel in China, the novel, with intricate plots, vivid description and characters, has a very high artistic value and an important place in literary history. The book has spread and spawned a variety of versions, some with 100 chapters, others with 120 and others with 70.

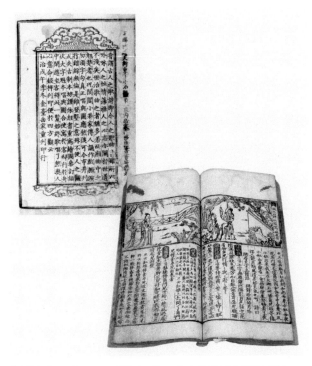

Journey to the West has 100 chapters and is based on the related story scripts of *Zaju* and the folklore of Xuanzang going on a pilgrimage for the Buddhist Scriptures. It was written by Wu Cheng'en (about 1504–1582) during the Ming Dynasty. The first seven chapters of the book

Jintai Yue's carving copy of *Qimiao Quanxiang Xixiangji* published by Beijing Book House in 1498.

deal with plots about the Monkey King, such as "Monkey King being born," "Making Havoc in Heaven" and others. The other chapters in the story deal with vanquished demons and monsters and overcoming difficulties in a pilgrimage for the Buddhist Scriptures with his three disciples Monkey King, Pigsy and Monk Sha. The book, very creative, with romantic descriptions, humorous language, great scope and complete structure, is a unique and outstanding piece of colloquial fiction.

A Dream of Red Mansions by the great writer Cao Xueqin (1715–1763) from the Qing Dynasty, takes the writer's family life as an archetype. With the love and marriage tragedy between Chia Pao-yu, Lin Dai-yu and Xue Baochai as its main plot, the book tracks the rise and fall of the prominent Chia family and reflects on the inevitable collapse of feudal society and the beginnings of democracy. The book, with an intricate plot, real life detail and elegant language is the greatest work of realism in ancient Chinese novels. The current popular version of the book has 120 chapters, the first 80 chapters of which were written by Cao Xueqin and the rest by Gao E.

The most outstanding colloquial short stories in the Ming and Qing dynasties are the *Three Collections and Short Stories*, namely *Yushimingyan, Jingshitongyan* and *Xingshihengyan* by Feng Menglong (*Three Collections*) as well as *Chuke Pai'an jingqi* and *Erke Pai'an jingqi* by Ling Mengchu (*The Short Stories*).

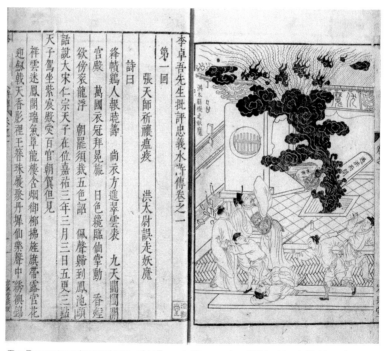

The Rongyutangs' carved copy of *Li Zuowu's Comment on "Water Margin"* in Hangzhou from the reign of Shenzong of the Ming Dynastry, whose imperial title was Wanli.

The former, with 120 selected story scripts, taken from unofficial histories or legends from the Song, Ming and Qing dynasties, reflects city residents' thought, life and interests and had a great influence on later colloquial fiction and drama. The latter, with 40 story scripts, integrates literary standards and language style.

The *Strange Tales of a Chinese Studio*, an outstanding representative of the classic Chinese novels of the Ming and Qing

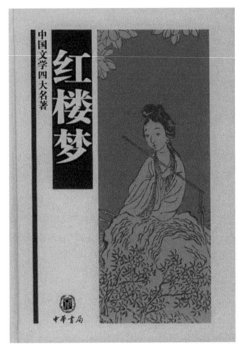

A Dream of Red Mansions published by the Zhonghua Book Company

dynasties by Pu Songling of the Qing Dynasty, includes 491 short stories, abundant subject matter and diverse content, most of which criticizes the darkness and corruption of society through stories about fox spirits and ghosts. The book, with bright and vivid figures and complicated and eccentric plots, successfully builds up numerous characters.

Encyclopedia of China

Chinese cultural circles have been always followed the fine tradition of compiling reference books. After the introduction of the modern encyclopedia, Chinese scholars, with several small and practical encyclopedias compiled in the early twentieth century, took to compiling a modern encyclopedia.

In 1978, the State Council decided to edit and publish the *Encyclopedia of China* and set up the Encyclopedia of China Publishing House to lead the work. By 1993, 74 volumes of all disciplines, with 126 million words, nearly 50 thousand pictures in 780 thousand entries, had been published. As a famous first edition, the *Encyclopedia of China* is for readers above the senior high school level. Its publication was hailed as "a monument of Chinese Culture" and it became a well-developed symbol of Chinese scientific and cultural undertakings.

According to common international practice, a new edition of the encyclopedia usually comes out at several-year intervals. Since the first edition of the *Encyclopedia of China*, many changes have taken place in China, which result in the need to constantly update knowledge in various fields. Work on the second edition of *Encyclopedia of China* began in 1995. After more than ten

The first edition of *Encyclopedia of China*.

years of work by the editorial committee and scholars around the country, the second edition was finished and published by Encyclopedia of China Publishing House.

Based on the first edition, the second edition of the *Encyclopedia of China*, adapted to the development and demands of the era, has had numerous entries edited, replaced and renewed.

With a total of 32 volumes (30 volumes of text and 2 for the index), 60 million words, 30,000 pictures and nearly 1,000 maps and 60 thousand entries, the second edition, is accurate, authoritative, readable and accessible. It is a systematic and comprehensive reflection of the latest developments in science and provides abundant reflection of significant achievements in the process of building socialism with Chinese characteristics. In addition, it is not only a set of practical reference books suited to public reading and use but also serves economic and social development and is the first large-scale modern comprehensive encyclopedia that conforms to common international practices in China.

Progression
The Modernization of China's Publishing Industry

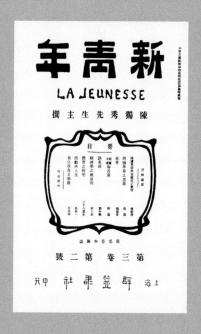

At the beginning of the nineteenth century, advanced publishing technology was introduced to China, heralding a profound transformation in Chinese publishing. After the Opium War in 1840, developed capitalist countries from the West broke China's isolation. At the same time, with the influence of capitalism, traditional Chinese society began to collapse. During the tremendous changes society and culture underwent, the traditional publishing industry entered into a transition period. The period marked a move for the Chinese publishing industry from the traditional to modernity, gradually establishing a solid foundation for modernization.

At the end of the nineteenth century and at the beginning of the twentieth, a large group of modern private publishing agencies such as the Commercial Press, Zhonghua Publishing House and Wenming Publishing House emerged. They symbolized the end of the transition of the Chinese publishing industry from traditional to modern. The differences in modern publishing match the development of Chinese society.

On the whole, the hundred years from the beginning of the Opium war in 1840 to the founding of the People's Republic of China was a significant stage for the rise and development of modern Chinese publishing. The period from the beginning of the twentieth century to 1949 was particularly prosperous. According to conservative estimates, from 1911 to 1949 at least 120,000 different books were published in China. There were more than 10,000 periodicals and magazines and 2,500 newspapers. The sheer number of publications was unprecedented in China's publishing history. Meanwhile, the rise of a modern publishing industry played an active role in promoting the development of Chinese society and culture.

The Introduction and Application of Mechanical Printing

The introduction of modern printing technology from the West facilitated the rise of modern Chinese publishing. By the early years of the nineteenth century, mechanized letterpress printing had been introduced in China and the Christian Protestant missionary Robert Morrison (1782–1834) from the London Missionary Society brought the first Chinese character font set to China. In 1814, he founded a printing shop in Malacca to cut matrixes of Chinese characters and cast types out of them. In 1819, a printed Chinese copy of *The Holy Bible—the Old Testament and the New Testament* was the first Chinese printed book and resulted in the first group of trained press operators.

Large electric printing machine used in the Zhonghua Book House at the beginning of twentieth century.

From the time of the 1840 Opium War, Western missionaries came to China and some of them began to do printing and publishing to facilitate their missionary work. In 1843, the British missionary Walter Henry Medhurst (1796–1857) moved his printing shop from Batavia to Shanghai and named it Mohai Book House. It was the first printing and publishing agency with letterpress printing machines in Shanghai. After the founding of the Mohai Book House, a number of publishing agencies set up by foreigners emerged, including Meihua Book House, Yinghua Book House and Gezhi Book House. The largest was Meihua, which also had the most advanced technology.

In 1879, a British businessman named Ernest Major (1841–1908) founded the Dianshizhai Printing House to print Chinese books by polyautography. The books printed by Dianshizhai were portable and popular, small in size with beautiful scripts and low prices. After that, polyautography became popular and a number of polyautography book houses were set up. Polyautography replaced block-printing as the most common printing form in China and helped set up profit driven printing agencies.

At the beginning of the twenthieth century, polyautography was replaced by type printing as the use of printing machines spread. Improvements and innovations were made for the new type of printing based on the unique features of Chinese characters. After this, developing in leaps and bounds, printing technology

The British missionary Robert Morrison, a pioneer translator.

Shanghai's Dianshizhai Printing House drawn by Wu Youru, a famous Qing Dynasty painter.

in China narrowed the distance with technology used in Western countries and moved from manual operation to mechanization.

After developing from the beginning of the nineteenth century to the twentieth century, modern machine printing became the mainstream of China's printing industry. Traditional printing technologies such as movable-type printing or block-printing and registration printing were left behind. With these fundamental changes in productivity, the printing industry gradually became an industrial enterprise and adopted capitalist operating models.

The transition to modern printing directly led to the transition of the traditional Chinese book system. Before the nineteenth century, thread-bound books were the most common in China. After the introduction of new printing technologies, paper imported from abroad also can into use. Statistics show that in 1903, the value of paper imported from abroad hit 2,684,000 taels of silver. By 1911, the value had jumped to 5,605,000 taels. From 1903 to 1911, a total of 34,165,000 taels of silver were spent to import paper. As a result, imported paper replaced cork paper and became the most commonly used. It also allowed for a shift from one-side printing to printing on both sides of the page.

In addition, there were changes in binding and layout as Western styles overtook most publications. Popular in the West, hardback and paperback books began to be widely used in China, marking a transformation in book binding and layout.

The Rise of New Publishing Houses

After the nineteenth century, the traditional publishing system started to decline and collapse. At the same time, modern profit-driven publishing houses emerged, developed and promoted the development and reform of society in unprecedented ways.

Missionaries and foreign merchants set up publishing agencies with capitalist features. These enterprises provided examples and guided the modernization of China's publishing industry. The most famous were the Mohai Book House, Yinghua Book House, Meihua Book House, The Christian Literature Society for China and the Shanghai Newspaper Press, among others. These publishing agencies used advanced publishing strategies, technology and management imported from the west and promoted the transition of China's publishing from traditional to modern.

After the rise of the "Westernization Movement" in the 1860s, influenced by new publishing agencies of the West, the Qing Dynasty government established translation schools and official book bureaus comprising the Translation Department of the Jiangnan Arsenal, the Beijing Translation School, The Jinling Book House, the Zhejiang Book House, the Jiangsu Book House and others. These new organizations were markedly different from the traditional official publishing industry.

Modern web press that uses different types of paper.

From the end of the nineteenth century to the early years of the twentieth century, the general mood of society in China changed and private publishing agencies emerged. In 1882, Xu Hongfu and Xu Run set up the Tongwen Book House in Shanghai, the first private modern publishing enterprise founded by Chinese with private funds. After that, a group of private modern publishing enterprises like the Feiying School, Hongwen Book House and Jishi Book House emerged. At the same time, some traditional private book houses changed themselves into modern publishing agencies.

The founding of the Commercial Press in 1897 marked a new development stage in China's modern private publishing. In 1906, the first book industry chamber of commerce was set up in Shanghai with twenty-two new publishing agencies as members. After the founding of the Commercial Press, many new private publishing agencies sprung up, such as the Zhonghua Book House, Civilization Book House, World Books, Dadong Book House and Kaiming Book House. Market-oriented and guided by modern publishing concepts, these book houses used modern machine-printing and resorted to various and flexible modern operation models to fulfill their social responsibility as publishers, while maximizing their commercial profits. They became the mainstay of modern Chinese publishing and led to a new prosperity in modern Chinese publishing.

Among the numerous private publishing agencies, the Commercial Press and Zhonghua Book House are the most influential and have the longest history. In 1936, 9,438 books were published and republished. Of those, Commercial Press published 4,938 books and Zhonghua Book House published 1,548. These two presses published 6,486 books, or 69%, of all the books in the country.

Commercial Press and Zhang Yuanji

The Commercial Press was established by Xia Ruifang, Bao Xian'en, Bao Xianchang and Gao Fengchi and others in Dechangli, Jiangxi Road in Shanghai in 1897. At the beginning of the twentieth century, in step with the New Culture Movement that advocated vernacular writings, the Commercial Press edited and published many books about new ideas and emerging culture. Besides introducing Western learning and publishing versions of Chinese classics, the Commercial Press also edited and published many textbooks and copies of ancient books. More importantly, it trained plenty of editorial staff that went on to found or to lead some famous publishing agencies early in the twentieth century. The Commercial Press went from being a small printing house to become the largest new publishing enterprise in the history of modern China, mostly thanks to the leadership of Zhang Yuanji.

Zhang Yuanji (1867–1959) was originally from Zhejiang Province. He was a famous sinologist, historian and the most influential publisher in modern history. In 1920, at the invitation of Xia Ruifang, Zhang Yuanji joined the Commercial Press. He regarded the development of education as his duty.

In 1903, he took over the post of director of the communication and translation institution of the Commercial Press. He took over as manager in 1916. By 1926 he had become president of the press, a post he held until his death. During his fifty-year publishing career, Zhang Yuanji made outstanding contributions to the modern publishing industry, culture and education.

As a great publisher with groundbreaking ideas and well versed in both Chinese and Western cultures, Zhang Yuanji was erudite, well-informed and insightful with a strong patriotic passion and a sense of social responsibility. Taking advantage of the emergence of new learning and the abolishment of the

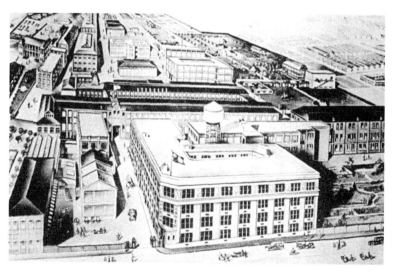

A restored modern panorama of the Commercial Press, which grew rapidly and became the largest press in the Far East in the twentieth century.

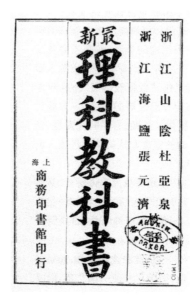

Zhang Yuanji

The title page of the *Ideal Textbook*, part of a series published by Commercial Press

imperial civil examination system by the Qing Government, he formed a team to write and edit new textbooks.

Under Zhang Yuanji's leadership, the first textbook for primary schools was published in 1904. The book broke new ground in the history of modern Chinese education. After that first effort, textbooks published by the Commercial Press became popular across the country. Zhang Yuanji also devoted himself to introducing Western cultures and bringing new knowledge into China. He carefully chose and organized the translation and publication of a large group of academic and literary classics from abroad. Among them, the *Origin of the Species* translated by Yan Fu (1854–1921) and *La Dame aux Camellias* translated by Lin Shu, had profound influence.

He also set up the East Library and the Hanfenlou Library and made use of the resources in more than fifty official or private libraries to print 610 books and 20,000 volumes by photo-offset, including *Sibucongkan, The Histories of Twenty-four Dynasties* and *Xuguyi Series*. Beautifully printed, these unprecedented versions were complete and became examples for later generations. The Commercial Press also edited and published lots of reference books. In 1915, the first new dictionary *Ci Yuan* or *Chinese Etymological Dictionary* was published. The press also published many well-known periodicals such as *The Magazine of the East, Novel Monthly, Education, Women, Students* and others.

During the Second World War, the Commercial Press was destroyed. Zhang Yuanji formed a committee to revive the press and wrote a slogan that underlined his enthusiasm, and that of the country's, for new publishing ventures: "Sacrificing for the country and striving for culture." He continued printing in Chongqing and other places.

Zhonghua Book House and Lu Feikui

In the history of modern Chinese publishing, the Zhonghua Book House, established in 1912, enjoys fame equal to the Commercial Press. Its founder was Lu Feikui, who was from

An institution of the Zhonghua Book House.

Zhejiang Province. He was well educated and had plenty of publishing experience. He led the Zhonghua Book House for almost thirty years, during which time the book house published more than 4,000 different books.

Textbooks published by Zhonghua Book House.

In its first year of operation in 1912, fixed capital was only 25,000 RMB. By 1916, the printing house's capital had reached 1,600,000 RMB and the book house became the second largest private press in the country, behind the Commercial Press.

The house had a number of significant types of publications. Textbooks were the most important. The publishing house put out more than 400 different textbooks, which were considered the best in the industry in the years of the Republic of China. The second most important type was social science books. There were more than one thousand different social science books edited and published by the book house. Among them, *Culture Series*, *Social Science Series* and so on were most popular. The third type was magazines. The book house published more than twenty magazines, among which *The Great Zhonghua*, *Education in Zhonghua*, *Novels in Zhonghua*, *Students in Zhonghua*, *Children in Zhonghua*, *Women in Zhonghua*, *Zhonghua English Weekly* and *Zhonghua Children Pictorial* were most famous. The fourth type was reference books. The *Zhonghua Great Dictionary* was published in 1915, *The Compendium of Works of Past and Present* printed by photo-offset and *Words Encyclopedia* published in 1936 were the most famous. The fifth type was ancient books, which were rearranged and reprinted. The *Ju Zhen Fang Song Version of the Histories of Twenty-four Dynasties,* published in 1930, and the *Ju Zhen Fang Song Version of Si Bu Bei Yao,* printed in 1930, were best known.

The Emergence of New Publications

After the nineteenth century, with the rise of modern publishing, the content and type of publications in China changed greatly.

Books focused on modern disciplines

Confucian classics, history, philosophy and literature are the main categories of traditional Chinese books. After the 1840s, China opened up to the outside world gradually with increasing contact with the West. As a result, intellectuals broadened their horizons and began to learn about and to introduce western culture and thoughts. At the same time, many translated books were published to spread the new knowledge, which led to

The Chinese scholar Hua Hengfang (1833–1902) and his translated version of *Elements of Geology*.

fundamental changes in the content and structure of publications. Besides Confucian classics, many books on history, philosophy, literature, many natural sciences, applied science, philosophy and social science were published and many new disciplines were established. More than 120,000 different books in eighteen categories published from 1912 to 1949 were collected in *The Title Catalogue in the Years of the Republic of China*, comprising philosophy, psychology, religion, politics, law, military, economy, culture, science, education, sports, literature, arts, medicine and health, agricultural science, communication, transportation and others. Based on these classifications, by 1949, the system of modern disciplines had almost reached maturity.

Newspapers and magazines published on a massive scale

With the great expansion of content for publication, various new publications came into existence. Newspapers and magazines were published on a large scale. *The Title Catalogue of Chinese Periodicals of China* shows almost 20,000 Chinese

The first Chinese periodical was set up in 1833 in Mainland China. It was called *East and West Study Monthly*.

periodicals in fifty libraries across China, which were published at home and abroad from 1833 to 1949. *The Catalogue of Collected Chinese Newspapers Published before the Founding of the PRC in Shanghai Library* records more than 3,500 different Chinese newspapers, published at home and abroad from 1862 to 1949. In addition to reporting the news, modern newspapers and magazines promoted the development of modern publishing and mass media and exerted great influence on society.

Textbooks, new reference books and pictorials

From translating versions of foreign textbooks to editing and writing by Chinese scholars, from textbooks written in classical Chinese to those written in the vernacular, textbooks experienced a process of continuous transformation to meet the needs of the times. This evolution was partly based on the sheer variety of publications, including traditional books, category books and title catalogues, as well as a group of reference publications edited and published quickly, such as newspaper and periodical indexes, dictionaries, tables, chorographic maps, annuals and handbooks. Pictorials were created on the basis of novels with illustrated portraits of the main characters - pictures were more important than words. These new publications were popular among readers as soon as they were published.

The Social Transition Promoted by New Publishing

Modern ideas filter into people's minds

From the nineteenth century, publishing concepts from the West were introduced into China as Western learning spread eastward. The concept of "freedom of the press" was one of the most important.

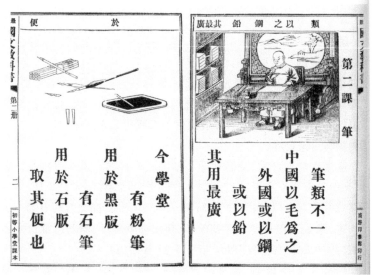

The text from the *Latest Version of Chinese Textbook for Primary School*, printed in the early twentieth century by the Commercial Press.

In 1644, the idea of freedom of the press was first proposed in *Areopagitica*, written by British political commentator John Milton. A rising capitalist class used the slogan "freedom of the press" as a weapon to strive for democracy. Something similar happened in China. From the mid-1800s, freedom of the press not only became a weapon to criticize and fight against feudalism, but also an ideal and a pursuit for reformists from the capitalist class. In 1912, after the success of the revolution of 1911, the government of the newly founded Republic of China declared in *"The Provisional Constitution of the Republic of China"* that "people enjoy freedom of speech, writing, press, assembly and association," meaning that freedom of the press was a right protected by law.

The establishment of copyright

The concept of copyright protection gradually made its way to the hearts of the people, promoting the establishment of a

Different magazines focusing on western learning published in China towards the end of the nineteenth century.

Dian Shi Zhai Pictorial published in 1887: "A crowd of people were looking on a giant from the west."

modern copyright system and the promulgation of copyright law. In 1903, the Commercial Press signed the first modern publishing contract in China, with the famous translator Yan Fu for his translation of *A General Theory of Society*. The contract read that both the translator and the publisher shared the copyright of this book. If the contract became invalid, the copyright would be left with the translator. The translator could not allow other publishers to print this translation work unless the contract became null and void. Both the translator and the publisher's rights and obligations were specifically identified by the contract that bound and protected both sides, facilitating the enforcement of the copyright contract, which was originally devoid of substance.

The establishment of the copyright system in the early years of the twentieth century not only meant that Chinese writers could enjoy their due rewards, but also showed the acknowledgement of and respect for writers' rights by society at large. Laying the economic foundation for the growth of writing as a profession, the copyright system directly promoted an increase in the number of writers and allowed for the continuous prosperity of publishing and cultural causes.

The promotion and development of society

Society was relatively closed and stable in China before the nineteenth century. Although some changes had taken place through the introduction of Buddhism and then the Western learning that came to China at the end of the Ming Dynasty, no fundamental transformations had taken place. This had a profound influence on traditional Chinese publishing, which developed in a closed but stable way.

After the nineteenth century, a dramatic transformation took place in China due to the influence from foreign countries and a tendency towards modernization. Under these conditions, China's publishing industry was forced to begin its modernization and became a barometer for the fate of the country and its people. In the course of this transition, ideas such as "save the country from doom and strive for national salvation" and "advance with the times" were given priority by the publishing industry. Lots of books on modern natural science and social science were published to spread new thoughts and scientific knowledge, which provided a strong impetus for the development and transformation of Chinese society.

At that time, four types of publications exerted a positive influence on Chinese society. The first was reading material to spread modern scientific and cultural knowledge through new textbooks and new translations. The second was works to publicize revolution among the people. Third was cultural and artistic reading material meant to elevate people's souls and

New Youth magazine, which published "A Study on Sport" by Mao Zedong in his youth.

enrich their lives. The last type was ancient books and other reference books to preserve national cultural heritage.

After the 1840s, through the publication of books and magazines, different social classes and political groups publicized their political ideas and various cultural and scientific ideas from the west spread through these books. It can be said without exaggeration that the most significant political movements in this period and the introduction of Western culture on a large scale were closely connected with publishing activities, which served as a catalysts in social transformation.

For example, the works of Charles Darwin translated by Yan Fu caused a sensation and the idea of "survival of the fittest in natural selection" influenced several generations. During the early years of the twentieth century, a set of books used to publicize the need for revolution was published to meet the needs of the times. They contributed to the success of the Revolution of 1911. The spread of advanced ideas such as democracy, published in some publications including *New Youth,* could be credited with facilitating the rise of the New Culture Movement in 1919.

The interaction between publishing and society laid a solid foundation for the development of contemporary publishing. It is necessary to note, however, that although traditional publishing is no longer popular, it did not die out completely with the advent of modern publishing.

Carrying Forward the Cause and Forging into the Future

The Prosperity of Chinese Publishing in the Contemporary Era

From the founding of the People's Republic of China in 1949, as an important part of the cause of "socialism with Chinese characteristics," Chinese publishing has made remarkable achievements. With the deepening of reforms and opening-up to the outside world, Chinese publishing has played a more and more significant role in the construction of the economy and culture as well as in cultural exchanges between home and abroad. The achievements made during the past sixty years prove that China has become a world-class publishing power.

The Scale of Publication

Since the founding of the PRC, publishing in the mainland has made great strides, although it has experienced some twists and turns. Especially after the adoption of reforms and opening-up to the outside world in 1978, Chinese publishing made outstanding achievements, best illustrated by the following statistics: In 1950, there were 211 publishing houses across the country and 12,153 books were published with total print runs of 275 million. In 1978, there were 105 presses and 14,987 books were published with the total print runs of 3.774 billion. In 2008, there were 579 publishing houses that put out 274,123 books, 7.062 billion volumes and 56.113 billion actual print runs.

The number of periodicals has increased from over 600 in 1977 to 9,549 in 2008, while that of newspapers has increased from 200 in the past to nearly 1943 in 2008 with 44.292 billion pieces. Circulation numbers for audio-visual products and electronic publications in 1978 were over 30 million pieces; while in 2008, 11,721 audio products were published in 254 million boxes; 11,772 video recording were published in 179 million boxes; the number of electronic publications published hit 9,668 with 157,706,400 units. The Chinese publishing industry has already achieved a historic shift from a shortage of cultural output to a surplus, from a single medium to diverse forms that meet people's various and multi-layered spiritual and cultural needs.

China's publishing industry has made great contributions to the economic development of the country and has had great social benefits. According to statistics from the General Administration of Press and Publication in 2004, the added value of the publishing industry was RMB193.97 billion, accounting for 1.7% of GDP in 2004 and 5% of the added value of the tertiary-industry. In 2008, the total price value of books and periodicals reached RMB129.68 billion, the sale value of publications was RMB162.28 billion and total sales for the printing industry surpassed RMB97.69 billion.

In addition, according to predictions made by the research group of the Chinese Institution of Publishing Science in "A

Children choose books at the Xinhua Book Store on the eve of Child's Day.

Study on the Development Index System of the Publishing Industry in a Well-off Society," by 2020, the added value of the Chinese publishing industry will reach RMB800 billion, accounting for 1.9%–2.0% of GDP. Publishing has become a significant part of the national economy, playing an increasingly important part in the promotion of economic and social development.

The strength of presses in China has grown with the development of publishing groups. There are currently some twenty-five publishing groups in China. They have become the most organized producers of published materials in Chinese publishing history. In 2006, publishing groups put out more than 40% of the total number of books printed and accounted for more than 30% of the value of all books sold and 30% of

The well-known author of many best-sellers, Yi Zhongtian, shakes hands with young readers. More than three million volumes of his *Comment on the Three Kingdoms* have been sold.

the total number of books published in China. The books published by publishing groups account for over one third of all books published in China. Meanwhile, among the many publishing groups, the most powerful, the China Publishing Group, represents the development of Chinese publishing in the contemporary era.

Aiming to meet the needs of reform and development in the publishing industry, the China Publishing Group, a national large-scale publishing institution, was established on April 9th, 2002 with China Publishing Group as the parent company. The company is made up of fourteen subsidiaries including the People's Literature Publishing House, the Commercial Press, Zhonghua Book Company, Encyclopedia of China Publishing House, China Fine Arts Publishing Group, People's Music Publishing House, SDX Joint Publishing Company, China Translation and Publishing Corporation, Oriental Publishing Center, Modern Education Press, Xinhua Bookstore Head Office, China National Publications Import & Export (Group) Corporation, China Book Business Report and Rongbao Zhai Press. It contains holding companies, mutual shareholding companies and affiliated companies including Zhongxinlian Corporation, Zhongbanlian Corporation, Digital Media Company of China Publishing Group. The Group is a large-scale enterprise that integrates publishing and marketing, chain-operations, import and export trade, copyright trade, printing and reproduction, information technology services, scientific research and development and fundraising, participates in national publishing plans, national publishing awards, the retail market, mass publication sales, the export and import of publications and so on.

The exhibition area of the China Publishing Group during the sixteenth
Beijing International Book Fair in 2009.

With 9,800 employees, the group has total capital of RMB6.5
billion and sales income of RMB3.9 billion per year. It turns out
more than 10,000 kinds of publications including books, audio-
visual products, electronic and online publications as well as
forty-seven types of periodicals and newspapers every year. It
has a 7% market share in the domestic publication retail market
and makes more than 1,000 copyright deals every year.

The group, the country's largest import and export publication
company, exports and imports more than 200,000 various
publications every year, accounting for 62% and 30% of the
trade in books and periodicals respectively. The group also
owns twenty-seven overseas presses, book chainstores and
administration bodies with business in more than 130 countries.

Publishing Technology Advances: the Rapid Development of Digital Publishing

In terms of the history of publishing, the progress of the industry has been driven by reforms and transformations in publishing and printing technology. Since the 1980s, advances in Chinese publishing and printing have narrowed the gap with the most advanced in the world and have given momentum to the development of contemporary Chinese publishing.

In July 1981, the first Chinese character laser editing and composing system, Huaguang I, was tested at ministry level. Chinese character laser editing and composing technology helped the Chinese publishing industry enter into the new age of "light and electricity" and end the age of "lead and fire." Its inventor Wang Xuan has been praised as the "Bi Sheng of modern China."

Wang Xuan (1937–2006), the inventor of the Chinese character laser editing and composing system.

(Bi Sheng was the inventor of movable-type printing technology in ancient China.)

After this, laser editing and composing technology was upgraded and color laser editing and composing invented. It is thought that 99% of presses and printing factories in Mainland China use this technology. Since 1991, presses in Hong Kong, Macao and Taiwan have also used it, including Ta Kun Pao of Hong Kong, the Macao Daily News and Taiwan's Central Daily News. This system has also been introduced to other countries such as Malaysia, the US, Canada, Thailand and Japan. The system allows for faster composition and production, saves manpower, financial and material resources and facilitates the digitalization of the entire publishing process, laying a foundation for Chinese publishing to keep up with its overseas counterparts.

Digital readers exhibited during the Frankfurt Book Fair in 2009.

The rise of new media technologies, such as internet networks and mobile phones, provides a further environment for the development of Chinese digital publishing. By the end of September 2009, there were 360 million internet users in China, a popularization rate of 27.1%. The number of users of the mobile internet was 192 million and 99.33 million people used broadband internet. The expansion of basic Internet resources saw the number of IP addresses hit 123 million, the second largest in the world. Total domain name registrations were the highest in the world at 5 million.

In terms of the scale of the market, in 2008, the output value of the internet industry was nearly RMB150 billion. The output value of IT, production, software and the digital industries was RMB200 billion. According to the statistics, in 2009, the total number of mobile phone users exceeded 700 million.

With plenty of new media equipment available, many literate people have the necessary technology to read new media with products such as the Apabi Reader by the Founder Company, the Hanwang E-Book and the Chinese On-line E-Book. These digital publications have large reader groups and a large market share.

Over the past few years, the scale of digital publishing has grown with an improved industrial chain and various publishing forms. As network and digital reading become important reading forms, e-books, publishing on demand, mobile phone publishing and blogs begin to play an important role in Chinese publishing. In 2002, the value of digital publishing was RMB1.59 billion; by 2008, it had multiplied to RMB53 billion.

Based on "The Report on the Development Trend of Chinese E-Books in 2007," there were 660,000 e-books published and more than 300,000 were in widespread circulation. The number of readers on the market was 59 million and total sales income in 2007 reached RMB169,400,000. Sales income of five publishing houses in 2007 hit RMB5 million, while 10 others sold more than RMB4 million.

Recently, the rapid development of digital publishing has pushed traditional publishing to speed up its transformation. At the end of 2008, 90% of presses had launched e-book publishing business and published 500,000 different e-books with the income from them reaching RMB300 million. Some 300 newspapers had some kind of digital newspaper business, with 9,000 kinds of digital periodicals and annual sales of RMB760 million.

The Commercialization of Publishing

To satisfy the needs of economic development and international competition, changes have taken place in China's press and publication system and reform has become fast and intensive in the past years. Presses are divided into two types, to either meet the public interest or for profit.

Publishers have gradually become companies and put in place modern operations that adhere to the law. "The Enforcement Program on the Deepening Reform of Publishing and Distribution System" stipulated by the General Administration of Press and Publications in 2006, encouraged publishing and distribution groups to hold stock from each other and take part in mergers and acquisitions. It also encouraged non-public capital to enter into industries approved by various policies.

In October 2006, Shanghai Xinhua Media Co. Ltd. became the first press company in China to go public. After that, Sichuan Xinhua Winshare Chainstore Co. Ltd. was listed on the Stock Exchange of Hong Kong. On December 21st, 2007, the Liaoning Publishing and Media Co. Ltd. went public in the Shanghai Securities Exchange, becoming the first state-owned cultural

Established in 1937, the Xinhua Book Store has become a well-known brand with the largest book sale network in China.

enterprise with an editing and publishing business to go entirely public and become the top stock in China's publishing and media industry.

As of 2007, twenty-three publishing groups began to enter the capital markets actively through mergers and acquisitions. Reforms have been carried out in more than 100 bookstores and Xinhua Book Stores had undergone commercialization in twenty-nine provinces, autonomous regions and municipalities directly under the Central Government. Some of those stores have implemented a shareholding system.

Chain operations have been implemented in twenty-three provincial Xinhua bookstores. Five book logistic centers with a floor area of more than 100,000 square meters were set up in China. The annual profits have reached millions of RMB. There were eight national private chain companies and the number of distribution

新华书店
XINHUA BOOKSTORE

图书
BOOK

同一个世界
One World

世界 同一个梦想
World One Dream

The Beijing Book Building, located in the crowded downtown of Xidan, Beijing, is one of the largest book retail markets in China.

companies reached 100,000. There were more than fifty Sino-foreign joint ventures, Sino-foreign cooperation or foreign-invested distribution companies focused on books and periodicals. A network of distribution companies has grown rapidly and nine publishing and media companies have gone public with market capitalization of RMB200 billion and net financing of RMB18 billion. All these developments indicate that publishing companies in China have undergone profound changes.

"The Guidelines on Further Promoting the Reform of the Press and Publication System" was issued by the General Administration of Press and Publication in April 2009, which presented a more specific route map and schedule for the reform of the press and publication system. It was regulated in the guidelines that, except for those in public welfare and institutes of higher learning, engaging in profit-driven books, audio and video products and electronic publications, must complete the work of transforming into enterprises by the end of 2009, and those of the departments and commissions under the central leadership by the end of 2010.

With the rapid marketization of publications, laws affecting press and publications have improved. In 1990, the "Copyright Law of the People's Republic of China" was promulgated, it took effect in 1991. In the same year, the "Regulations for the Protection of Computer Software" were approved by the State Council. In 1992, China signed the Berne Convention and the Universal Copyright Convention, which marked the improvement of the publication law system of modern China and the integration with copyright efforts around the world. After that, the promulgation of laws for the Chinese publishing industry sped up. In 2001, to promote and meet the rapid development needs of the publishing industry, the Standing Committee of the National People's Congress passed the "Copyright Law of the People's Republic of China."

Also in 2001, the State Council approved and promulgated the "Regulation on Publication Administration," the "Regulation on the Administration of Audio-Visual Products" and the "Regulation on the Administration on the Printing Industry." In 2008, the "Regulations for Administration of Publishing Electronic Publication," "Regulations for Administration of Making AV Products," the "Regulations for the Administration of Book Publishing" and the "Regulations on the Administration of the Occupational Qualifications of Publication Technologists" formulated by the General Administration of Press and Publication took effect.

On April 21st, 2009, the "Regulation on Legislative Procedure of General Administration of Press and Publication" was approved at the first meeting of the General Administration of Press and Publication. It was to take effect from June 1st, 2009. Today, a system of publication with law at the core and based on administrative regulations has been created in China, shaping a law-enforcement system that has played an active role in the protection of the development of Chinese publishing.

Professional Education and Research

High quality talent is the foundation for the rapid development of the publishing industry, in which changes have taken place in terms of employment structure and quality. From 1978 to 1997, the annual rate of increase of employees in the industry was 11%. From 1998 to 2008, the rate reached 16%.

Meanwhile, education and research in publishing has grown fast, providing theoretical guidance and talented employees for the publishing industry. From the 1980s, a complete professional education system of publications for multiple disciplines, levels and channels has been formed. Until 2008, undergraduate editorial and publication programs have been available in more than seventy universities or colleges. More than forty universities or colleges now offer postgraduate programs and ten offer doctorate level programs. In terms of publication research, from 1977 to 1980, a new upsurge in the establishment of research institutions has been evident in different provinces, cities, autonomous regions, and fourteen printing technology institutions have emerged.

In 1985, approved by the State Council, the China Institute of Publishing and Distribution was set up (which changed its name to the Chinese Institute of Publishing Science in 1989). After that, different types of publishing research organizations have been established one by one and a network of publishing, printing, periodicals, newspaper, media and copyright research was gradually formed.

Many academic exchanges, such as the International Publishing Symposium and the Annual Meeting of Chinese Edition Science are held frequently. Every year, many academic achievements are made. In 2008, 425 monograph textbooks and 38 types of periodicals were published. In addition, professional academic networks comprising the Network of Chinese Press and Publication, the Network of Chinese Publishing and the Publication and Academic Network have become new platforms of academic exchange.

Publishing Industries in Mainland China, Taiwan, Hong Kong and Macao: Chinese-Language Publishing

While the publishing industry in China has developed rapidly, those of Taiwan, Hong Kong and Macao have also undergone great developments. The pattern of "diversity in unity" of Chinese-language publishing has been based on the joint

The Macao exhibit in the Frankfurt Book Fair in 2009

development of publishing in the mainland, Taiwan, Hong Kong and Macao.

At the Chinese-language publishing forum at the Frankfurt Book Fair in 2009, the Vice-Director of the General Administration of Press and Publications, Wu Shulin, stated in his key-note speech "Jointly Create a Bright Future for Chinese-language Publishing by Enhancing Tradition and Exerting Advantages," that Chinese-language publishing boasts a great cultural tradition. This tradition is based on research, drawing lessons

The Taiwan exhibition at the Frankfurt Book Fair in 2009

from history, recording scholarship and seeking perfection, publishing organizations supported and supplemented by the government and ordinary people, the continual renovation and innovation of printing technology and open-minded exchanges.

Chinese-language publishing has enjoyed development based on rich resources from Chinese civilization, the current scale and experience of Chinese-language publishing in the mainland of China, Taiwan and Hong Kong, and huge market demand at home and abroad. In the near future, Chinese-language publishing in mainland China, Taiwan, Hong Kong and Macao will experience greater development and will play an increasingly significant part in the global publishing industry.

The Road of Books
Interaction between Chinese Publishing and the Outside World

The growth and development of Chinese civilization cannot be separated from its extensive exchanges with multiple civilizations. The ancient Chinese were passionate about learning all they could from foreign civilizations. At the same time, Chinese civilization spread to every corner of the world and promoted the spread of Confucianism. In these bilateral exchanges, the spread of publishing became significant.

As the well-known Silk Road emerged, so did the "Road of Books." Through this road, China shared papermaking and printing techniques with the rest of the world, while disseminating ancient science, technology and culture. In the same way, foreign science and technology were also introduced to China, which in turn, had a huge impact on Chinese society and culture. The interaction between China and the outside world facilitated the development of Chinese publishing over the centuries.

The Spread of Papermaking Techniques

Paper was already popular in China at a time when many other countries and peoples continued to use ancient and primitive writing materials. For example, Indians used palm leaves to transcribe scripture, Egyptians and Europeans used papyrus, vellum and wax tablets.

As a medium for language, paper has unparalleled advantages. After the invention of papermaking in China, it not only spread domestically but also found its way to foreign countries and, in a very short time, replaced local media and promoted the development of local publishing and cultural undertakings.

Initially, what was exported was paper and paper products such as books, letters and paintings. Later, it was the

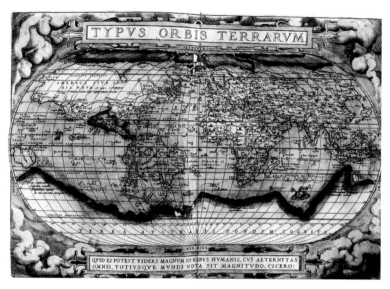

Theatrvm Orbis Terrarvm, compiled and prepared by Belgium cartographer Ortelius Abraham, was published in Belgium in 1570 and was the earliest European world map introduced to China.

papermaking technology itself. The first recipients of paper were China's neighbors such as Korea, Japan and other countries in Southeast and South Asia. In the second century, Chinese manuscripts were exported to Korea and in about the third century, the papermaking technique was introduced there and in Vietnam. From Korea, Chinese books were exported to Japan. In 610, the Korean monk Tanzheng introduced papermaking to Japan. In the seventh and eighth century, it was introduced to India. For example, during the Tang monk Yi Jing's stay in India (671–694), the word "paper" already existed in Sanskrit. These countries, upon assimilation of this skill, gradually exported their paper products to China, which promoted economic and cultural exchanges.

Paper and papermaking spread to the Western world through sea and land. Around the second century, paper was brought to western cities like Heicheng, Dunhuang, Tunufan and Loulan. In the fifth century, paper was used across the central Asia region. In the eighth century, papermaking was introduced to the West. In 751, in a war between the Tang and Dashi (the Abbasid empire) in Talas (near Taraz in today's Kazakhstan), the army led by the Tang general Gao Xianzhi (?–756) was defeated and thousands of Chinese soldiers were captured. Some of them were paper makers who introduced this technique to the Arabs in Samarkand (now Uzbekistan), which had rich hemp and flax resources. A papermaking mill was established. Soon paper became an important Arab export to the west. This story was recorded in Arabian historical books. For example, the famous Arabian scholar Thaalibi (961–1038) once said that "of the specialties produced in Samarkand, what is worth mentioning is paper. It is neat, cheap and suitable, so it replaced Egyptian papyrus and vellum. And such paper only existed here and in China." The author of the book *Journey and Kingdom* says paper was introduced by captive Chinese. These prisoners were owned by Ziyad, the son of Salibi. Some of them knew how to make paper. The production of paper not only met local demand and became an important commodity in trade, it met global demand.

Later, between the eighth and the

A scene from a medieval European parchment workshop.

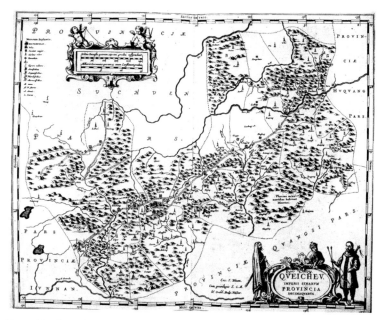

Novus Atlas Sinensi, prepared by European missionary Martin Martini, published in the Netherlands in 1655, the earliest map of China published in the west.

twelfth century, Arabs established paper mills in Baghdad, Damascus, Egypt and Morocco. In 1150, Arabs reached Spain and established the first European paper mill in Xativa, in the north of Spain. By then, the papermaking technology improved by Cai Lun had existed for over 1,000 years. At this time, the only people who had mastered papermaking in Spain were Arabs and they monopolized the technique for four-hundred years. It was not until 1189, when the French established their own papermaking mill, that mills emerged in Christian countries.

Between the thirteenth and the sixteenth century, many countries including Italy, Germany, the Netherlands, England and Russia built paper mills. In 1575, the first American paper mill was built in Mexico. In 1690, the first North American paper mill appeared in Philadelphia. It was not until the nineteenth century that Melbourne, Australia, had its first

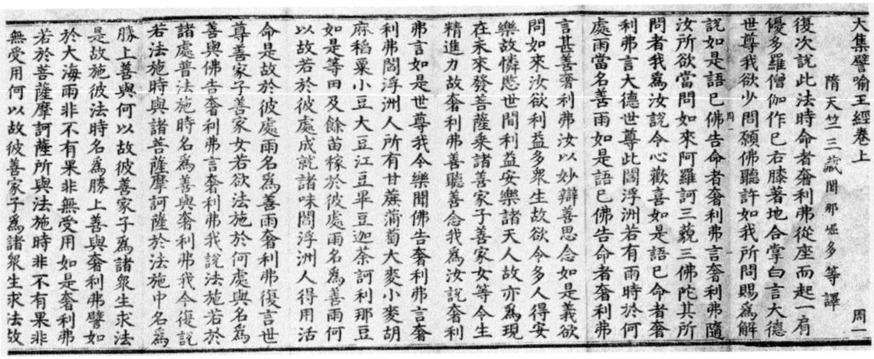

大集譬喻王經卷上
隋天竺三藏闍那崛多等譯

復次說此法時命者奢利弗從座而起一肩優多羅僧伽作已右膝著地合掌白言大德世尊我欲少問願佛聽許我所問賜為解

說如是語已佛告命者奢利弗言奢利弗汝所欲當問如來阿羅訶三藐三佛陀其所問者我為汝說令心歡喜如是語已命者奢利弗

利弗言大德世尊此閻浮洲若有兩時於何處兩當名善兩如是語已佛告命者奢利弗

言甚善奢利弗汝以妙辯喜思念如是義欲問如來汝欲利益多眾生故令多人得安樂故憐愍世間利益安樂諸天人故亦為諸菩薩乘諸善家子善女等令生

在未來發菩薩心故樂故憐愍世間利益安樂諸天人故亦為諸菩薩乘諸善家子善女今生

精進力故命者奢利弗善聽善念我為汝說奢利弗

弗言如是世尊我今樂聞佛告奢利弗言奢利弗閻浮洲人所有甘蔗蒲萄大麥小麥胡

麻稻粟小豆大豆江豆畢豆迦茶訶利那豆如是等同及餘苗稼於彼處兩名為善兩時

以故若於彼處成就諸味閻浮洲人得用活

令是故於彼處兩名為善兩奢利弗復言世尊善家子善女若欲法施於何處與名為

諸菩薩訶薩時與諸菩薩訶薩言奢與奢利弗我說法施奢若於

若法施時與彼善家子為諸眾生求法故是故施彼法時名為與奢利弗善上善與何以故彼善家子為諸眾生求法故

勝上善與何以故彼善家子為諸眾生求法故

無受用何以故彼善家子為諸眾生求法故若於菩薩訶薩所行法施時非不有果非無受用何以故

周一

Yongle Beicang, printed by the imperial court in 1440, with concertina binding and standard script.

paper mill. Over around 1,000 years, Chinese paper had spread around the world.

Once papermaking was introduced to Europe, local people attempted to improve the technique. Even in the seventeenth century, their skill was equivalent to that of the Song Dynasty. To address the problem of poor-quality paper, the French Minister of the Treasury, A.R.J. Turgot (1727–1781), wanted to use Jesuits stationed in Beijing as spies to learn from the Chinese. In Emperor Qianlong's reign, the French missionary Michel Benoist (1715–1774), who was working in the imperial court, secretly copied the Chinese papermaking technique and sent the details back to Paris, which led to the spread of advances in Chinese papermaking. In 1797, the Frenchman Louis-Nicolas Robert successfully invented machine papermaking. This was the first time that Western papermaking technology overtook China's technology.

The Spread of Printing in Other Countries

China was the home of printing. When this great invention emerged, it soon spread to neighboring countries and later to

West Asia, North Africa and Europe. Printing technology in most countries came from China, directly or indirectly. Some was built on the inspiration of Chinese printing.

Printing spread first in Asia. It was used to print Buddhist sutras and the *Tripitaka* in particular. Korea, Japan, Vietnam and some other countries with long friendships with China and influenced by Chinese culture, used Chinese characters widely and followed Buddhism. As a result, the printed *Tripitaka* became a most precious gift to these countries. Later, what was printed in China was not enough to meet their needs, so they learnt to print themselves, which helped spread printing techniques. Still under Chinese influence, printed books in these countries bore distinctive Chinese style. This did not change until the rise of modern printing.

Korea

Korea was among the first recipients of Chinese printing. In the seventh century, Korea often sent students to China, who returned with many books. Books were also exported to Korea as gifts or commodities, mostly Buddhist sutras. Chinese printing was introduced to the Korean Peninsula thanks to the spread of Buddhism. It is difficult to determine the actual year this happened due to an absence of historical records, but a reliable estimate is the eleventh century.

In 993, at the request of the Korean kingdom, the North Song Kingdom gave the Buddhist Canon of the Kaibao Era as a gift to the country. It was also probably during this time that Chinese type carving went to the Korean Peninsula. Later, some people were sent by Korea to China to learn woodblock printing. They later became the first printers in Korea. Between 1011 and 1082, Korea reproduced the *Tripitaka* for the first time.

After Bi Sheng's invention of moveable-type block printing, Koreans learnt this technique through his description in the

Ancient copper-printing type from Korea exhibited in Gutenberg Museum of Germany

Dream Pool Essays (*Mengxi Bitan*). They built on this when they tried other innovative approaches such as using soil type, wood type, copper type, lead type and iron-moveable type to print books. The most successful invention was copper type, which contributed to the spread and application of printing technology.

Japan

There is a very long history of exchanges between Japan and China. In 645, the Taika Reform in Japan started a wave of learning from China. Many envoys, monks and students were sent to China to learn Confucian culture and advanced technology. They returned with many articles, including copies of printed editions.

Woodblock printing was introduced to Japan through this process. It is said that around 770 copies, some 1 million volumes of the *Mantras of the Dharani Sutra* were printed and preserved in ten temples, where they are still kept today. Since these books do not have the date of printing, some Japanese scholars believe the printing was possible because of Chinese printing technology. The earliest block-printed book with a recorded date in Japan

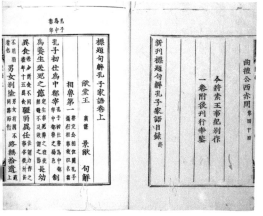

The School Sayings of Confucius printed with moveable type in Japan.

Wood types from the Japanese Enkoji Temple.

was the *Doctrine of Mere Consciousness* in 1088, which was based on books from the Song Dynasty. Wooden and copper types were also used in Japan. Of the books printed in Japan, a large proportion was of Chinese origin and their content was similar to the Chinese originals.

Vietnam and Southeast Asia

As early as *the* Song dynasty, Chinese books were introduced to Vietnam in the form of gifts, such as printed *Tripitaka* and *Daozang*. Early printed books in Vietnam often dealt with Buddhism. The earliest recorded printed articles were household residency records printed between 1251 and 1268. In 1295, Vietnam received a Chinese-printed *Tripitaka* and later reproduced this book.

In the 1430s, the Vietnamese government started to print Confucian classics. In the seventeenth century, Chinese color registration was introduced. Print shops specialized in New Year painting also emerged in Hanoi and other places of Vietnam; the theme, content and techniques employed in these prints came from China. In the early eighteenth century, wooden moveable

Chongning Wanshou Tripitaka, printed between 1080 and 1103, the first private printing of *Tripitaka* in the world.

blocks were used to print books in Vietnam.

In the fourteenth century, many Chinese in southeast coastal areas went to do business or settle down in the south pacific region. They brought with them paper, ink and books. Some Chinese craftsmen started printing businesses in Southeast Asia, which roused local interest in printing technology and promoted its development.

Iran

Paper money, paper cards and religious printed articles were introduced to West Asia during the Song and Yuan periods. They had the greatest impact on Iran. In China, Iran was called Anxi. Along with Persia, it had economic and cultural exchanges with China via the Silk Road. Persians were familiar with Chinese printing. They printed and issued paper money, modeled on Chinese practice, in 1294. The money had Chinese

Printed paper card from ancient China

and Arabian characters on it. In his 1310 Great Universal History, the Persian historian Rashid al-Din Tabib gave a detailed description of Chinese woodblock printing, proving that Persians learned about printing from China. As a meeting place between East and West, Persia had many European merchants who also came to appreciate the significance, function and craft of printing.

Europe

With the westward movement of the Mongol armies, the link between China and West Asia, Central Asia and even Europe improved greatly and exchanges became more frequent. To pass time and to use as gifts back in Europe, many merchants bought Chinese paper cards. Throughout the Crusades, many new things were introduced to Europe from the east, including paper cards, print painting and images. Many historians have noted that the soldiers fighting in the Crusades brought oriental block-printing articles back to Europe.

Printed cards, paper money and religious paintings thus became the predecessors of printing technology in West Asia. The French sinologist Abel Remusat commented that the shape, format and size of early paper cards in Europe were identical to what was used in China. Most were hand painted. Though paper cards are small, they use various techniques such as hand painting and woodblock printing. They served as the most direct means for Europeans to learn the relevant technologies. What is more interesting is that because so many foreign paper cards were taken to Italy, the Venetian government had to issue a

The oldest existing wood print in Europe: *St. Christopher and Jesus*, from Germany.

directive prohibiting the import of printed articles from outside Venice in 1441. It has become a scholarly consensus that Chinese woodblock printing was introduced to Europe between the late fourteenth and early fifteenth century.

After the Europeans discovered woodblock printing, they soon found type carving to be very cumbersome and not suitable to the alphabetic language. Therefore, block printing became more common. By the late fourteenth century, wood and block-printed paper cards appeared in Europe. The earliest known wooden religious print in Europe was the *St. Christopher*

Early wood print *Book of Revelation* from about 1425

and Jesus of 1423. In this German painting, St. Christopher is carrying a young Jesus across a river holding a cross in his hand. The left corner has mill wheels from China and two lines under the carving to the effect that whenever you see this image you will be spared the fate of death.

Block-printed books first appeared in Europe in the 1440s. In terms of printing method, either words or images were carved in *intaglio* on a wooden block. A piece of paper was gently brushed on top of the ink-painted block. The similarity of technique and raw materials to Chinese counterparts suggests that European block printing was influenced by the East.

To Europeans, moving from woodblock printing to movable-type block printing was not very difficult. The later system was particularly well suited to the Latin alphabet. The Uighur ethic group in Xinjiang, China, who lived in the meeting place between Europe and Asia, had developed wooden Uighur Script moveable type suitable for alphabetic language as early as the twelfth century in the Turpan region. This system served as a reference for the transition of Chinese moveable type for use for an alphabetic language.

In the fourteenth century, many tourists, merchants and missionaries from Europe brought back information about moveable-type block printing from China, so wooden movable-type blocks appeared in Europe first. The Swedish scholar Theodor Buchmann (1500–1564) in 1584 described how wooden blocks were made in Europe: "Initially people carved all the words on one single block, which was very time consuming and costly, so later people used wooden moveable blocks, and then placed them together to make a block." Wooden moveable blocks were a major link to the transition to metal moveable block.

It was against this background that the German Johannes Gutenberg started an in-depth exploration. Inspired by wooden movable type, he developed moveable type suitable for the European alphabet in 1450 using an alloy made of lead, tin and antimony, which resolved the long-standing problem of European-language printing. He also invented a wooden printing press using screws to assert pressure on the plate, instead of purely manual operation, which greatly enhanced the quality and efficiency of printing. His invention quickly spread to various parts of Europe and transformed the situation from one in which only nobles and monks could read and receive higher education. It facilitated scientific advances and the emergence of the European Renaissance.

Karl Marx believed that the invention of printing, gunpowder and the compass were "a necessary precondition for the development of the bourgeoisie" and are of enormous and far-reaching significance to Europe and the world at large.

Exchanges between Domestic and Foreign Books

China was both an importer and exporter of books. Before 1840, China exported more than it imported, and was in the leading position in global publishing, particularly with countries and regions under the influence of Confucianism. The situation was reversed from 1840 onwards. Chinese publishing also declined in terms of printing. Under the influence of the western world, Chinese publishing underwent a major transformation in the late nineteenth century and enjoyed another period of boom.

China is the most advanced and influential Asian country in terms of printing. Since the third century B.C., cultural and economic exchanges between China and Korea, Japan, Vietnam, India and other Central Asian countries have been ongoing, and so was the exchange of books. For a long time, with the wide spread of Chinese culture, books from China were also exported in large volume to neighboring countries. This point has been analyzed above. The following part will focus on the introduction of Western books to China.

Among the foreign books that came to China, Buddhist classics represented the lion's share. They were also the most influential. In the first and second century, Indian Buddhism was introduced to China through the Silk Road, as were Buddhist sutras. Since then, massive translations of Buddhist scriptures began and the exchange in publishing between China and foreign countries also boomed. Gradually Buddhist sutras became a major category in Chinese books. Translations were continuous from the third to the tenth century. In 971, the first *Tripitaka* in Chinese was printed, which included 1,076 Buddhist classics in 5,048 volumes. This project was repeated in the following dynasties. By 1738, with the completion of Emperor Qianlong's version of *Tripitaka* (1,662 sections, 7,168 volumes), a total of seventeen Chinese versions of *Tripitaka* were printed in imperial China.

The introduction of Buddhism had a huge impact on Chinese printing. First, it promoted the development of translation. Second, it gave full play to the role of printing. Third, Sanskrit texts printed on narrow traverse paper sheets inspired the Chinese to move from the scroll-page format to album leaf format. Last, but not least, Buddhism spread to Korea and Japan through China. Under Chinese influence, the former also engaged in large-scale printing of Buddhist scriptures,

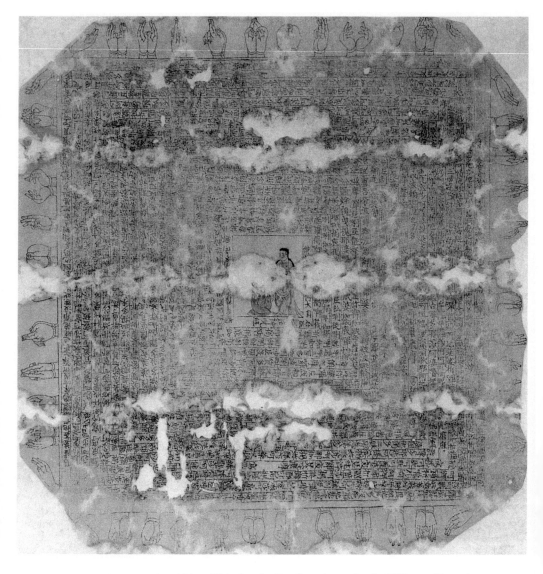

Chinese version of *Dharani Sutra* from the Tang Dynasty unearthed in 1975, one of the early Chinese printed materials.

Sutras in Mongolian language: *Fanjiazhuang.*

which promoted the development and exchange of culture and printing.

Western books were not introduced to China until much later. The translation of these books did not start until the late sixteenth century when a group of European Catholic Jesuit missionaries began making translations of their classics with which to preach. Between 1582 and 1757, over 500 missionaries came to China, and more than seventy participated in the translation of over 400 books. Most of these books were on religion and the others on natural science and the humanities.

The publication of *Veritable Records of Catholic Saints* by the Italian Father Michele Ruggieri in Guangzhou, in the year 1584 marked the beginning of foreign publication. From 1605, the Chinese scholar Xu Guangqi (1562–1633), working with Italian Father Matteo Ricci and others, translated over ten scientific works. Though what Matteo Ricci and other missionaries wanted from translation was evangelical, their efforts actually brought useful knowledge to China. For example, *Original Geometry*, a joint work by Ricci and Xu Guangqi, is one of the earliest Chinese

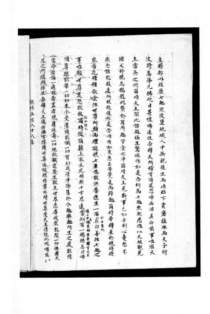

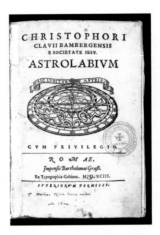

Christophori Clavii Bambergensis e societate Iesv, by Father Matteo Ricci, moveable-type printed Latin version in 1593, deposited in the China National Library.

translations of western natural science. *On Optical Tubes*, authored by J. A. Schall von Bell (1592–1666) was the first western book on optics introduced to China. The *Illustrated Explanation of the Entire World*, written by Ferdinand Verbiest (1623–1688) and the *Atlas des Nations* by Matteo Ricci opened the eyes of Chinese people to the world. The *Outline of the Human Body* and *Western Views of the*

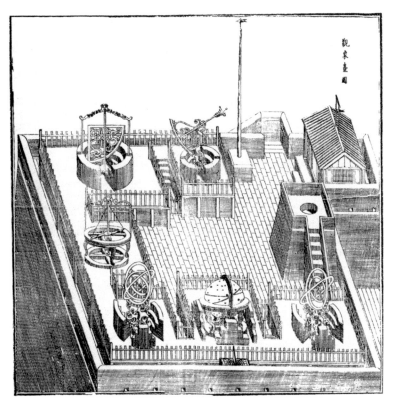

Liber Organicus by Ferdinand Verbiest, court edition from 1674, the thirteenth year of Kangxi's reign

Human Body translated by Johann Schreck (1576–1630) are among the earliest books on physiological anatomy that were introduced from Europe to China.

Bound by the theology, missionaries did not bring the most advanced ideas and science from Europe. However, they still introduced many fresh ideas to China. Unfortunately, in 1723 Emperor Yongzheng ordered that all the Western missionaries be expelled from China, closing the door to Western technical and scientific knowledge. For a long time, translation of these books came to a halt.

Book merchants in Qing Dynasty as described by Westerners.

Exchange in Modern Times

In the early years of nineteenth century, Western missionaries came to China again, bringing not only advanced printing machines to do publishing business, but also doing missionary works and introducing capitalist society through translating books. At that time, China's traditional publishing industry had declined. The arrival of missionaries heralded a new era in the translation of Western books and exchange between the Chinese publishing industry and that of the West:

1) Translation works were published on a large scale. Through books, Western thoughts and culture came into China on a large scale, exerting profound influence on the society and culture of China. New translation works were the main publications of the church, government and private publishing agencies, and

translation works became the most important publications in the Chinese publishing industry. According to statistics, during more than two-hundred years from 1528 to 1757, the type of books translated by missionaries in churches numbered more than 400; from 1850 to 1899, the number of translation works published in China reached 537; from 1902 to 1904, the number of translation works was 533 - equal to the amount of that published in the half of nineteenth century.

In addition, based on the Chinese scholar Xiong Yuezhi's statistics, from the first Western book translated by Robert Morrison and published in China in 1811 to the end of the Qing Dynasty in 1911, 2,291 types of Western books were translated and published in China, which lead to the long-lasting movement of Western learning spreading to the east. Centering on subjects such as "to know the world," "enrich and strengthen the country," "save the nation from doom and strive for its survival," "democratic revolution," "science and enlightenment," this movement had a profound influence on the transformation of society in China.

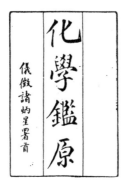

Translation works on chemistry published at the end of the nineteenth century in China.

The portrait of John Fryer, the Englishman who worked in the Translation Department of the Jiangnan Arsenal for the longest time in China.

2) Foreigners participated extensively in the Chinese publishing industry. Men such as Robert Morrison, William Milne and Ernest Major opened book companies in China; others, such as John Fryer, John Allen and Alexander Wylie, joined publishing agencies already established by the Chinese. They all made a great contribution to the development and transformation of the modern Chinese publishing industry. According to rough statistics, nearly sixty printing agencies were set up by Christian organizations and more than twenty by the Catholic Church. Meanwhile, lots of foreign employees worked in printing agencies set up by the Chinese, such as the Beijing Translation School, the Translation Department of the Jiangnan Arsenal, Foreign Languages School, the Commercial Press and so forth.

3) Some publishing agencies began to operate joint Chinese-foreign publishing. For example, the Commercial Press invested jointly with Japanese companies from October 1903 with 100,000

The written notes by John Fryer and the contract signed between him and the Jiangnan Arsenal.

Yuan invested by each part and 50% of the stock held by each part. The Commercial Press became the first Chinese-foreign joint company in the history of Chinese publishing, which played a significant role in the development of Commercial Press.

4) Chinese books and classics were introduced abroad. These books were brought into Britain, France, Germany, Russia, Japan, America, Sweden and Holland, and the main classics were translated into foreign languages and spread abroad. During the movement of "Western learning spreading to the East" the tradition of "Eastern learning spreading to the West" was also formed.

At that time, the breadth and depth of exchange between Chinese and foreign cultures through books was unprecedented. In the process of modernization, the Chinese publishing industry also developed unprecedented international features.

Copyright Trade and International Exchange

Since the founding of the new China in 1949, exchange between home and abroad in the publishing industry has become frequent. The copyright trade has developed rapidly for the past sixty years and especially during the years since the adoption of reform and opening-up to the outside world in 1978. In 1992, China signed the "Berne Convention" and "Universal Copyright Convention"; in 2003, matching the commitment which was made when China entered into the World Trade Organization, China opened up its printing industry and publication distribution service. In 2006, the distribution sector of the Chinese publishing industry opened in a comprehensive to foreign capital. By December 2007, the distribution of foreign enterprises approved by the General Administration of Press and Publication numbered 62, 24 of which were solely-invested enterprise, and 38 were joint ventures.

The copyright trade is the product of the establishment and improvement of the socialist market economy in China after the adoption of the policy of reform. Since 1978, the scale of trade of Chinese books has changed from small to large, with publishing agencies and others engaging in a major export trade. With the deepening of reforms and exchange with the outside world, the laws and regulations of copyright have improved gradually, and will be conducive to the development of the industry.

According to statistics, in 2007, 11,101 copyright publications were brought into China, 10,255 of which were books, 270 sound recordings, 106 video recordings, 130 electronic publications and 337 soft wares. 2,593 kinds of copyright publications were exported abroad, 2,571 of which were books, 19 sound recordings, and 1 electronic publication. The export trade of books and periodicals, audio-visual products, electronic publications has increased by 140%, 73% and 112% respectively, compared with those of 2001 before China's entry into the WTO. In 2007, the proportion between copyright import and export for the mainland of China was 3.99:1. Moreover, 16,969 kinds of publication copyright were brought into China and 2,455 types of publication copyright were exported in 2008. 15,776 types of book copyright were brought in, while 2,440 were exported, with the proportion between copyright import and export 6.47:1. Although still an unfavorable trade balance, it has improved. In

Founded in 1986, the Beijing International Book Fair (BIBF) has been held many times, becoming the fourth international publication fair in succession to the Frankfurt Book Fair, the American Book Exposition and the London International Book Fair. The picture shows the Beijing International Book Fair in 2007.

2008, the top ten areas and countries for book copyright import were: Taiwan, America, Britain, Japan, South Korea, Germany, France, Singapore, Canada and Russia. The top ten areas and countries for book copyright export were: Taiwan, South Korea, Singapore, America, Russia, Germany, France, Japan, Britain and Canada. The two lists indicate the breadth of the copyright trade.

On the whole, since 1995, the proportion of book copyright import and export has fluctuated. Before 2004 (except 1998 and 2002), the trade deficits of book copyright trade were above 10:1 with the highest 15:1. Since 2004, the deficits of copyright declined year after year, and in 2007 was 3.99:1, the lowest in the history, which can be seen from the chart below:

The total amount of book copyright import and export projects in China from 2001 to 2008

Year	Book copyright import	Book copyright export	Trade deficit	Import/ export
2001	8,250	653	7,597	12.63:1
2002	10,235	1,317	8,918	7.77:1
2003	12,516	811	11,705	15.43:1
2004	10,040	1,314	8,726	7.64:1
2005	9,382	1,434	7,948	6.54:1
2006	10,950	2,050	8,900	5.34:1
2007	10,255	2,571	7,684	3.99:1
2008	15,776	2,440	13,336	6.47:1

At present, China has actively imported advanced printing technology and copyrights from abroad, and continuously intensified efforts to introduce Chinese books abroad. Under the guidance of the policy of "help China go to the world and let the world know China better," the Chinese government has began to adopt the strategy of "going global". This has included "China Book International" and "the "Project for Translation and Publication of Chinese Cultural Works" held by General Administration of Press and Publication and Information Office of the State Council. Through providing translation subsidies, these two projects aim to encourage publishing agencies in different countries to translate and publish Chinese books and help people in around the world to know China better through reading books in their familiar languages. Recently, more than twenty countries and over fifty publishing agencies have applied for these projects for translation subsidy. With a continuous rise in the sales of publication abroad, China International Publishing Group and China Intercontinental Press have achieved a lot in terms of external publication.

For the past few years, the Chinese publishing industry has participated in different book fairs to publicize, exhibit and promote Chinese books. Activities held at international book fairs have become an important stage for the Chinese publishing industry to launch copyright trade and to publicize Chinese culture. After a Chinese publishing delegation took part in the Salon du Livre de Paris as guest of honor in 2003, China has also participated in the Moscow International Book Fair and Seoul International Book Fair as guest of honor respectively in 2007 and 2008. In 2009, as guest of honor of Frankfurt Book Fair, which is known as the "Olympics of the Publishing Industry," China demonstrated the 5,000-year-old culture of China to the world through the publishing industry and demonstrated the fundamental changes China has undergone in recent times. The activities held by China as guest of honor represented

The China section in the Frankfurt International Book Fair, 2009.

cultural exchange with foreign countries on the largest scale, to the highest standard and with the greatest influence of any held by the Chinese publishing industry in overseas since 1949. Some 272 publishing agencies from the mainland of China and 26 from Taiwan and 15 from Hong Kong, with more than 2,000 participators and 7,600 exhibitions, took part in the book fair in which 2,417 copyrights were exported. In addition, according to official statistics from Germany, more than 290,000 people visited the book fair, which promoted the Chinese publishing industry's effort to go global.

Among the various international book fairs, the annual Beijing International Book Fair, founded in 1986 and held every year since, has also played an active role in the promotion of the publishing trade and exchange between home and abroad. Guided by the policy of "introducing great foreign books to China and letting Chinese books go global to promote the international exchange of technology and culture and enhance the mutual understanding and friendship for all countries," the book fair is among the top four international book fairs with the greatest influence in the world, and is a great opportunity for Chinese publishers to strengthen communication and cooperation with publishers from other countries.

From 3-7 September 2009, the Sixteenth Beijing International Book Fair, with 43,000 square meters of exhibition area and 2,146 booths, was held. 1,762 publishing agencies from home and abroad participated in the fair with more than 160,000 kinds of exhibited publications. Over 1,000 activities were held in or out of the exhibition hall during the five days with more than 200,000 visitors. Spain, the guest of honor, with 1,000 square meters of exhibition area was a highlight of this book fair. Nearly seventy cultural exchange activities on the theme of "Dream of Spain, think of Spain, interpret Spain" were held, in which 30 Spanish publishing agencies, 15 writers, Chinese publishers and many readers participated. It was said that 12,656 agreements and contracts of trade copyright were signed, 11,264 of which were copyright intentions, 1,392 copyright contracts - an increase of 10.52% compared with that of the previous year.

In the future, the Chinese government will keep intensifying and expanding policy support for exchanges with other countries, and will encourage publishing enterprises from home and abroad to expand the scope and the field of cooperation. At the same time, the Chinese government will continue the campaign against copyright piracy and set up a copyright service system to create a sound environment for the cooperation of the publishing industry between home and abroad. It is predicted that, with the increasing contribution made by China to the world, the international level of the Chinese publishing industry will be elevated and China play an important role in the international publishing industry of the contemporary era.

Appendix I: A Brief Chronicle of China's Publishing

26th century B.C.: Appearance of Chinese characters.

21st–16th century B.C.: Appearance of primitive books and records.

1600–1046 B.C.: Beginning of primitive editing.

1046–771 B.C.: Government sets up specific book collections. Books and records appear.

770–256 B.C.: Private writing emerges. Confucius compiles ancient books and records.

213–212 B.C.: "Burning books and burying scholars alive"(*fenshu kengru*) by Emperor Qinshihuang.

2nd century B.C.: Invention of plant fiber paper for writing and painting. Early bookstores appear.

101 B.C.: Simaqian completed the first biographical style book *The Records of the Grand Historian*.

26–5 B.C.: The first large-scale state-level collection of books and preparation of state collection directory.

1st century: Introduction of Buddhism and Buddhist sutras to China. Buddhist scriptures translated.

105 AD: Papermaking improved by Cai Lun. Technique spreads across China.

175–183 AD: Carving of *Stone Classics of the Xiping Reign*, a large publication before the invention of printing.

7th century: Invention of woodblock printing, beginning of sutras and calendars using this technique. Bookshop and private printing emerges.

932–953: First government printing of the nine Confucian Classics and the first government-carved books.

971–983: First government printing of the Chinese version of the Chinese *Tripitaka*.

10th century: Invention of color woodcut printing.

1041–1048: Bi Sheng invents movable-type printing.

1048: *The Yongle Dadian Encyclopedia* is completed.

1561: Fan Qin encourages completion of *Tianyige*, the earliest known private book storage facility in China.

Late 16th century: Western missionaries involved in translation and writing in China.

1726: Compilation of *Gujin Tushu Jicheng* or *Complete Collection of Illustrations and Writings from the Earliest to Current Time*.

1782: Completion of *Siku Quanshu* (*Complete Library in Four Branches of Literature*).

Early 19th century: Involvement of foreign missionaries in Chinese publishing.

1840: Opium War starts. Western modern printing begins to penetrate China, leading to the reform and transformation of Chinese publishing.

1897: Founding of the Commercial Press, marking the emergence of modern private publishing.

1912: Founding of the Zhonghua Book Company, ushering in the modern publishing business.

1949: The 1st of October marked the founding of the People's Republic of China and a new growth period for the Chinese publishing industry.

1978: The "Encyclopedia of China" was launched.

1981: The first Chinese computer, Chinese character laser editing and the composition system Huaguang I was appraised at ministry-level, marking the Chinese publishing industry's entrance into the new age of "light and electricity" and the end of the age of "lead and fire."

1986: The first Beijing International Book Fair was held in Beijing.

1992: China signed the Berne Convention and the Universal Copyright Convention, which marked the improvement of the publication law system of modern China and the integration with copyright efforts around the world.

2009: As the guest of honor, China participated in the Frankfurt International Book Fair in Germany, which effectively promoted the Chinese publishing industry's effort to go global.

Appendix II:
Chronological Table of the Chinese Dynasties

The Paleolithic Period	c.1,700,000–10,000 years ago
The Neolithic Period	c. 10,000–4,000 years ago
Xia Dynasty	2070–1600 BC
Shang Dynasty	1600–1046 BC
Western Zhou Dynasty	1046–771 BC
Spring and Autumn Period	770–476 BC
Warring States Period	475–221 BC
Qin Dynasty	221–206 BC
Western Han Dynasty	206 BC–AD 25
Eastern Han Dynasty	25–220
Three Kingdoms	220–280
Western Jin Dynasty	265–317
Eastern Jin Dynasty	317–420
Northern and Southern Dynasties	420–589
Sui Dynasty	581–618
Tang Dynasty	618–907
Five Dynasties	907–960
Northern Song Dynasty	960–1127
Southern Song Dynasty	1127–1276
Yuan Dynasty	1276–1368
Ming Dynasty	1368–1644
Qing Dynasty	1644–1911
Republic of China	1912–1949
People's Republic of China	Founded in 1949